# SAVING PATRIOTISM

# OTHER BOOKS OF INTEREST FROM MARQUETTE BOOKS

Christine O'Brien and John Maxwell O'Brien, *Alexander the Great: A Lyrical Biography* (2022). ISBN: 978-1-17327197-4-3

David Demers, *The Killing of Bere Baudin: A Dystopian Novel* (2022). ISBN: 978-1-7327197-8-1

Tae-hyun Kim, Daniel Erickson, and David Demers, *How the Mass Media Really Work: An Introduction to Their Role as Institutions of Control and Change* (2014). ISBN: 978-0-9833476-9-9

David Demers, *Jelly Beans & Peanuts: Life and Times of Llewellyn Jenkins, an American Banker, Soldier and Family Man* (2014). ISBN: 978-0-9833476-8-2

John Wheeler, *Last Man Out: Memoirs of the Last Associated Press Reporter Castro Kicked Out of Cuba in the 1960s* (2009, Demers Books). 978-0-9816002-0-8

Tom Graves, *Crossroads: The Life and Afterlife of Blues Legend Robert Johnson* (2009, Demers Books). ISBN: 978-0-9816002-1-5

Charles J. Merrill, *Colom of Catalonia: Origins of Christopher Columbus Revealed* (2009). ISBN 978-0-9816002-2-2

John Schulz, *Please Don't Do That! The Pocket Guide to Good Writing* (2008). ISBN: 978-0-922993-87-1 (booklet)

Hazel Dicken-Garcia and Giovanna Dell'Orto, *Hated Ideas and the American Civil War Press* (2008). ISBN: 978-0-922993-88-8 (paper); 978-0-922993-89-5 (cloth)

Tomasz Pludowski (ed.), *How the World's News Media Reacted to 9/11: Essays from Around the Globe* (2007). ISBN: 978-0-922993-66-6 (paper)

Jami A. Fullerton and Alice G. Kendrick, *Advertising's War on Terrorism: The Story of the U.S. State Department's Shared Values Initiative Program* (2006). ISBN: 0-922993-43-2 (cloth); 0-922993-44-0 (paper)

Stephen D. Cooper, *Watching the Watchdog: Bloggers as the Fifth Estate* (2006). ISBN: 0-922993-46-7 (cloth); 0-922993-47-5 (paper)

Ralph D. Berenger (ed.), *Global Media Go to War: Role of Entertainment and News During the 2003 Iraq War* (2004). ISBN: 0-922993-10-6

Melvin L. DeFleur and Margaret H. DeFleur, *Learning to Hate Americans: How U.S. Media Shape Negative Attitudes Among Teenagers in Twelve Countries* (2003). ISBN: 0-922993-05-X

# SAVING PATRIOTISM

American Patriotism
in a Global Era

George R. Nethercutt, Jr.

Copyright © 2022 George R. Nethercutt Jr.

All rights reserved. No part of this publication may be reproduced, stored in a retrieval system, or transmitted in any form or by any means, electronic, mechanical, photocopying, microfilming, recording, or otherwise, without permission of the author.

Printed and Distributed by
Ingram Book Company of La Vergne, Tennessee

ISBN FOR THIS EDITION
978-1-7327197-2-9

Cover design by Jane Floyd of JF Design
Interior design by Marquette Books

Published by

**MARQUETTE BOOKS**
16421 North 31st Avenue
Phoenix, Arizona 85053
509-290-9240 (voice and text)
books@marquettebooks.com
https://MarquetteBooks.com

TO
MY DEAR WIFE OF 45 YEARS

# Contents

Preface, 9

Acknowledgments, 13

1 – Defining Patriotism, 15

2 – The Elements of Patriotism, 27

3 – Essentials of Patriotism, 53

4 – Dissent is Patriotic, 59

5 – Defining Civics and Its Elements, 74

6 – From Civics to Patriotism, 91

7 – How Citizenship and Patriotism Grow, 98

8 – A Legal Immigrant's Story, 106

9 – An Undocumented Immigrant's Story, 115

10 – History of Citizenship and a Recommendation, 120

11 – A Call to Patriotic Action, 134

Conclusion, 147

Endnotes, 151

Index, 167

About the Author, 174

# Preface

This book is about patriotism. I wrote it because I'm concerned that the words "patriotism," "patriotic," and "patriot" are used frequently, yet because civic learning has waned in America, most Americans understand neither the meaning of the words nor how vital patriotism is to our democracy. I spent ten years in Congress (from 1995 to 2005) and am convinced that not only is the average American not versed in American history, economics, government, or foreign policy, but neither are many of our nation's leaders. My goal in writing this book is to both educate and advocate for the civic knowledge of all Americans through a better understanding of the word *patriotism*.

This book is intended for Americans of all ages, particularly those interested in what patriotism means to a democracy in general, because patriotism has been de-emphasized in America for decades now by schools and some teachers — schools seem to focus more on STEM (science, technology, engineering, and math) subjects than civics. It's a book for millennials and Gen Zers, many of whom may lack fierce patriotism and civic knowledge if they haven't felt the pangs of war as their forebears have. In other words, some millennials do feel patriotic. This is also a book for older generations — to iterate what patriotism was, what it is today, and what it should be in the future.

Though I offer several viewpoints on the topic in the following pages, the perspective I most emphasize is what could be described as a traditional one, from loving parents who instilled in me healthy values such as integrity, kindness to others, and unselfishness. At its core, patriotism can be defined as love of country and pride in referring to oneself as an American.

Patriotism is not nationalism (the idea that America is perfect or Americans are part of an undying devotion to country), nor is it the implementation of the concept of one's country being "right or wrong." This perspective does not dwell on the challenges that poverty and other hardships pose to patriotism. Rather, it focuses on the importance of qualities such as honesty, respect for others, kindness, integrity, and selflessness — on the importance of comfort, not luxury; of statesmanship, not recreance; of humility, not arrogance; on those qualities that have been diminished in our culture.

In my family, there was mutual respect between parent and child, and I know I was loved. In turn, I was cognizant of the importance of upholding these family values when I went out into the world. These values help define the patriotism that is the essence of this book.

Some may call this perspective elitist, arrogant, or clueless, but it's the perspective and the values I was raised with, the perspective that helped me understand and appreciate the meaning of patriotism. People who have suffered racism, sexism, poverty, or family unrest may have a different definition of patriotism, one forged by their experiences. This book aims to include different perspectives, to look at the American experience and understanding of patriotism through the eyes of a broad cross section of America: from both legal and "illegal" immigrants, prominent individuals and those who have led ordinary lives, athletes and nonathletes, and people from different generations. They all bring varying and compelling perspectives worth thinking about and, in many cases, emulating.

Patriotism is a critical element in the perpetuation of the constitutional republic that is America. All Americans should understand and respect the country's system of government. Arguably, naturalized citizens — those who apply to the American government and must pass a civics test, among other requirements that are noted in this book — sometimes have a greater appreciation for America than many native-born Americans. Indeed, those born into American citizenship seem too often to take it for granted. Many are unable to name their local, state, and national public officials or don't understand how America came to be, and often they choose not to exercise their fundamental rights.

The beauty of American freedom is that citizens are free to worship God or not, to vote or not — to be patriotic or not. It's fundamental to American democracy. Freedom is what draws new citizens to the United States and influences them to seek naturalization. Freedom allows us choices: a hallmark of the American system, something our forefathers insisted upon and something generations of Americans have relied upon. Litigants have fought all the way to the US Supreme Court to assure the freedoms we enjoy today. Freedom is part of the American psyche. It's a patriotic sentiment that Americans have stressed for decades, and that's why citizens become outraged when others try to restrict their freedom.

This book will focus on patriotic actions both past and present and why these actions are so important. One way for all of us to become better citizens is to understand the struggles that Americans have undergone to protect our rights and keep our country's democracy true to the founding fathers' ideals. The struggle to preserve American values is a story of triumph and tragedy, of setbacks and successes, of struggles and accomplishments. Some of those triumphs and tragedies will be focused on here so that readers can appreciate the sacrifices our forebears made and the battles they fought to secure our freedom.

It's difficult to expect all Americans to view patriotism the same way: traditionally, like I do. Mark Twain once said, "I love my country but distrust my government." Loving one's country is a common denominator of all forms of patriotism. That doesn't preclude us from expressing ideas to improve it, however. Perhaps it's instructive for all Americans, regardless of social or economic position, to stand back periodically and reflect on the blessings they possess — and that others don't — as they strive in their own way to improve the United States.

As Peruvian novelist Mario Vargas Llosa said in a 1991 address at the Democracy Commission conference in Nicaragua, patriotism "represents a moral and emotional commitment to the web of historical, geographical, and cultural references that frame the destiny of every individual." This book will explore it all, hopefully increasing patriotic feelings and, in the end, helping everyone define their meaning of patriotism.

Thank you for considering this important national topic.

## Acknowledgments

Many thanks are in order for this book. Morgan McVicar, a writing teacher and friend I met at Harvard University, was indispensable to the effort. My dear wife of forty-three years, Mary Beth, read and reread my writing, always offering constructive and valuable advice. Our wonderful adult children, Meredith and Elliott, were patient and offered timely, modern thoughts. Ted McGregor, publisher and owner of the *Pacific Northwest Inlander* newspaper, was a fabulous and indispensable editor. Jayne Floyd of JF Designs was extraordinarily professional in beautifully designing the cover, and Marquette Books, owned by Arizona's Dave Demers, was gracious and thoughtful. Caroline Clouse of New York was essential. She did a wonderful job of editing and is a real pro where that skill is concerned — I could not have written this book without her help. All in all, I had a great team of professionals helping me.

CHAPTER 1

# DEFINING PATRIOTISM

*"Patriotism is a thing of the heart. A man is a patriot if his heart beats true to his country."*
–Charles E. Jefferson

Lucy, believed by some anthropologists to have been among the oldest humans of record, walked the ancient earth with fellow tribal members in Africa. The world's first humans were tribal in nature, parts of smaller units devoted to the perpetuation and survival of the "family." Lucy's skeletal remains were discovered in the 1970s.[1] She and her family members are believed to have originated from East Africa, thought to be the cradle of human civilization, where human skeletons estimated to be 3.6 million years old[2] have been recovered.

Other anthropologists believe Ardi was the first female to dwell on Earth, 4.4 million years ago near Ethiopia's Afar Desert.[3] And many biblical scholars trace the beginning of humankind to God's creation of Adam and Eve.

Whether Lucy or Ardi or Adam and Eve were first, humans have for many millennia joined together in a spirit of pride in their tribes, families and, later, communities and countries. Patriotism, therefore, can be defined as the coalescing of human beings in support of something greater than themselves — a tribe, a country, a nation-state — that they are devoted and committed to and want to make better.

For centuries, it has seemed only natural to love one's country. Patriotism has been celebrated in nations across the globe. In the United States, we need only think of patriots from Nathan Hale to General Douglas MacArthur to understand what the word has meant here for so many years.

Being a patriot, to most Americans in decades past and many still today, has meant being a good citizen; to love one's country and be attached to it; to know the country's history, its state capitals, what the branches of government are and how they work together; to vote in elections, work hard at our jobs, pay our share of taxes, volunteer, and participate in our communities. To be a patriot has meant to sacrifice, in battle or at home, when America has gone to war; to support the decisions of our government and have pride in our country's history and culture.

Former Army secretary and New York congressman John McHugh (R-NY), in an interview in 2018 with me, said that he sees great patriotic spirit in those who are part of the US military since they "live" their patriotism each day they serve their country. Representative Cathy McMorris Rodgers (R-WA) echoed John's sentiment in a similar 2018 interview, believing that military personnel are great examples of patriotism because each day, in doing their job, they support the patriotic mission of the United States — that is, a love of country.

Patriotism can be further defined as a "vigorous attachment to a homeland." Patriotism creates a sense of duty, of belonging to, and being devoted to, something bigger than ourselves, of accepting the concept of "all for one and one for all." Patriotism has been linked to national values, a devotion to one's country, and common support of a nation's policies.

But today, a host of factors — from the turbulence of the 1960s, the 1970s Vietnam War, and the rebellion of that era to the wars in Iraq and Afghanistan, Wall Street excesses, and globalization's elimination of borders — have changed the way many people view America and how they think of the words *patriot, patriotism*, and *patriotic* — words that are frequently used but without a clear and common understanding of what they mean.

Our telephones are assembled in China, some of our local newspaper stories are reported from India, and many of our domestic services, ironically, are from other countries. Are we citizens of the United States or citizens of the world? And, more importantly, how does the way we answer that question affect the notion of patriotism? Do most millennials and Gen Z citizens consider themselves Americans or are they disconnected from their country of birth? The argument can be made, though, that too many Americans, particularly among the younger generations, are citizens of *no* country, no continent, and no world. Too many can't identify Arizona or Nebraska, Iraq or Brazil on a map. They can't identify their US representatives or senators or how long a senator's term is, what the Battles of Bunker Hill or the Bulge were about, what the Supreme Court does, or who was president during World War II.

One popular YouTube video shows an interviewer asking ten random American University students in Washington, DC, to "name one US senator." Only one of them could, but all ten knew the hit song from the movie *Frozen*.[4] In 2011 *Newsweek* asked one thousand Americans to answer the basic questions on the US civics test for naturalization — the one applicants for citizenship must study and know (they must answer correctly 6 of 10 questions asked orally by an immigration officer). Too many didn't have any understanding of the Constitution. Even though all high-government officials must raise their right hands and swear to "preserve, protect, and defend" the Constitution, one must wonder how many of them have actually read it.

Too many Americans have not studied the past, are ignorant of the present, and are uncertain about the future. Their patriotic feelings are empty. Civic engagement is disappearing across America. Civics has not been comprehensively taught in our schools for at least a generation, though that's slowly changing. Some states now require high school seniors to pass the civics test for US immigration to graduate.[5] Other states require only about one semester of civic learning, often disguised as American government or American politics. That's hardly a comprehensive and dedicated study. A CBS/*New York Times* poll in 2012 found that 75 percent of Americans display the American flag at home or at work, up from 58 percent two years earlier. A 2017 American Enterprise Institute poll found that most Americans do consider themselves strongly patriotic.[6] And in 2020, a Gallup poll found that 63 percent of Americans described themselves as "very" or "extremely" proud to be American.[7]

Clearly, there's a disconnect between Americans' love of country and what they know about it. Citizenship and patriotism are connected, though. To add to the ample evidence of our civic illiteracy: in the *Newsweek* citizenship test challenge, 29 percent of respondents couldn't name the vice president and 73 percent didn't know why the Cold War was fought.[8]

*Newsweek*'s exercise was merely a recent gauge of Americans' lack of knowledge about basic history, economics, government, and foreign policy. Fewer Americans than ever, especially younger generations, keep up with politics; fewer than ever vote (except in 2008)[9]; and fewer follow the news online or in print. Many Americans have no concept of government's impact on them or on others.

Lack of civic knowledge is not entirely a new phenomenon,

though. Thomas Jefferson once declared, "My God! How little do my countrymen know what precious blessings they are in possession of, and which no other people on earth enjoy!" Still, Jefferson's compatriots lacked the internet and presumably could name their president and vice president and had some acquaintance with the Declaration of Independence.

In 1998, the National Assessment of Educational Progress (NAEP) showed that three-quarters of the fourth, eighth, and twelfth graders tested "lacked an understanding not only of American government but also the workings of civil society." Thirty-five percent of high school seniors tested below "basic," showing near-complete civic ignorance. The NAEP civics assessment is (according to their website[10]) intended to show students' civic knowledge and skills in terms of a set of achievement levels, defining basic, proficient, and advanced performance for each grade tested. The Civics Framework is a product of the "National Standards for Civics and Government," a voluntary product produced in 1994 by the Center for Civic Education.[11]

The 2012 NAEP scores suggest that, of four children in most American elementary school classrooms, only one will be proficient in civics. Among fourth graders, only one in four were able to identify the purpose of one of America's most famous documents — the US Constitution. A mere two out of ten eighth graders knew the role of the Supreme Court in American life.

The reasons for Americans' declining knowledge about America's past and present are fairly obvious: so much seductive media, cynicism, and apathy among adults. Meanwhile, partisan political, philosophical, and moral battles over what should be taught in schools led to the elimination of one thing after another, to the point in recent years of the disappearance of civics courses from American education. The fact that Americans are now polarized philosophically more so than in the past is evident from national polling data.[12]

Viewers now watch only those television channels with which they agree. Readers subscribe to newspapers or other publications with which they agree philosophically, not to expand their minds to opposing opinions, but to cement their preconceived notions. Their friends are like-minded. Whether on health care, North Korea, or immigration, Americans are deeply divided. Gallup finds that the internet has helped foster an angry and loud dialogue that has only exacerbated the divides within America on a broad array of social and political issues.[13] President Donald Trump won the 2016 election by playing on the anger across America.

Why our lack of civic knowledge matters is less readily apparent. Why does it matter whether 80 percent or 20 percent of Americans vote; whether we know what our local, state, and federal governments are up to; or whether we know who wrote the Gettysburg Address, what Jim Crow laws were, or what "Stonewall" signified?

There are many reasons knowledge of our history and political system matter, not the least of which is an undeniable connection between civic knowledge and civic engagement: studies show that citizens with a workable understanding of the American system of government are more likely to vote,[14] and it stands to reason they'd be more active in community affairs, volunteer in their communities, and engage in the respectful discussion and debate of political issues. Their families are likely stronger units. They can educatedly discuss public affairs at mealtimes. People are more likely to be patriotic if they're armed with knowledge of America.

Civic learning has waned over the last generation largely because America's schools have not heavily focused their attention on it, instead focusing more on STEM education. Those skills are important, but not at the expense of civic education. Two Harvard

University professors a few years ago opined that colleges and universities are shortchanging parents and college students because they haven't linked pure science and math to the social consequences or benefits of each scientific or mathematical finding or discovery. College professors have a duty to help students understand that pure science and pure math findings have social consequences and a connection to broader learning. The college professors were courageous to raise the issue. Those findings and their social connections should be explored in college classes. Only then can young people understand the linkage of one to the other.

History shows that affirming the connection between civic knowledge and patriotism is also necessary for the long-term health of any society. Citizens who know about their country and its history and who follow political events are much more likely to participate in civic affairs and have an interest in public policy developments. As more citizens engage in the formation of public policy through self-knowledge, more discussion occurs naturally among the citizenry, and hopefully compromises and consensus result and fair public policies are accepted. Such consensus may not satisfy all, but more will feel a part of the governance process and will avoid a sense of helplessness in facing a large national government. If the founding fathers hadn't been willing to compromise, the Constitution may never have been adopted.

Our Constitution has only been amended twenty-seven times, whereas other countries periodically and routinely rewrite their constitutions when leaders change (e.g., Zimbabwe, Rwanda, and China). Perhaps the survival of the American Constitution is evidence of America's greatness and of its lasting values, which together have resulted in the perpetuation of our national system.

Civic knowledge results in patriotic feelings and actions. It empowers and entices people to learn more about local, state, and national affairs; to understand their stake in what happens in Albany, Annapolis, or Juneau, as well as Washington, DC; and to identify and defend their interests in the political process.

The aftermath of the tragic school shootings in Parkland, Florida, in January 2018 showed powerfully how civic knowledge can be employed in a way that exemplifies how a democracy is supposed to work. Many of the surviving students gathered together and studied and debated gun control. They confronted their government leaders with reason, intelligence, and knowledge, not only of the gun control debate, but of how government works — or doesn't work. Florida students did research, learned the American system, worked with their legislators, and changed the law. Civic learning with a purpose led to real changes in Florida's law.

Ignorance of civics breeds fear, mistrust, and apathy. Knowledge breeds trust, understanding, and participation. Today, it's almost impossible not to engage in discussions about national policy, national leaders, or national affairs. People who say they aren't political are making a broader statement — they're affirming their political interests by remarking about their lack of political interests. It's impossible not to be political because there's always an issue that can stir people.

While they may not want to argue, there's always "something" or some issue that fires up their political juices. Too often, though, Americans socialize only with those who think as they do — they're communicating in an echo chamber.

The good news is that the political culture is becoming wise to the need for civic learning. The White House led a 2012 effort to identify the civic learning problem in colleges. It published, with broad input, "A Crucible Moment," a government call to action for colleges and universities to focus on civic learning as a core requirement for all college students and throughout the American education system. A 2012 conference at Harvard University assembled students from twenty-three colleges and universities to discuss how to better engage college students in civic activities.

A convocation of civic leaders gathered in Washington, DC, on September 21, 2017, at the invitation of prominent civic learning organizations and former US Supreme Court Justice Sandra Day O'Connor's iCivics organization, which focuses on teaching junior high school students about the American justice system and other civic learning issues. Indeed, civic learning is gaining bipartisan support. Liberal former Representative Jim McDermott (D-WA) and conservative Congressman Greg Walden (R-OR) both support civic learning.

Representative Denny Heck (D-WA) and Senator Ben Sasse (R-NE) have spoken publicly of patriotism. It's doubtful that any sitting member of Congress would declare civics or patriotism unimportant to Americans. Numerous groups that attended the conference emphasized the importance of civic learning to democracy. Identifying the steps necessary to get us there will ensure the perpetuation of our nation's democratic ideals.

The precarious future of patriotism speaks to the need for a national civics summit consisting of the best of government and the private sector to increase national engagement on civic learning. It should incorporate businesses and industries that have a stake in the civic learning outcome.

The broader goal is to ignite a national call to action to glorify civics and patriotism — for ordinary citizens and American leaders at every level — to insist on a civic learning resurgence for Americans of all ages. English writer G. K. Chesterton, a noted political thinker of the nineteenth and twentieth centuries, once wrote, "Education is simply the soul of a society as it passes from one generation to another." *Wall Street Journal* columnist Peggy Noonan has declared, "Glory exists only if you pass it on."

Patriotism, fostered by strong civic knowledge, can be a lasting legacy one generation passes on to the next, ensuring that our democracy — and our country — remain vibrant and true to the glorious heritage for which so many have fought. But it doesn't happen without greater focus and attention.

Civility and civics go hand in hand. While many have spoken out about the coarseness of Americans today, both in and out of politics, civility — treating others and their ideas with tolerance and respect — has in many respects disappeared. Today it's more popular to "get in someone's face" if you disagree with them, or to be aggressive with your political argument. That must change too, because coarseness only serves to polarize Americans more, highlighting our differences rather than finding where Americans can agree.

Today, when social activists "shut down" a political foe from speaking, the direct ramifications are that Americans are unable to grow and learn from that person. Rather than shutting down a thought leader so that no one even hears a controversial point of view, tolerance says to listen carefully to all speakers, whether you disagree or agree with the person. If done, all citizens will get into the habit of being more tolerant, a trait that leads to better citizenship. Millennials and Gen Z individuals may not have been exposed to war like their elders. Connecting one generation with another will help each understand the other better through the expression of positive behavior.

After the 9/11 tragedies, Democratic and Republican lawmakers gathered on the steps of the US Capitol and sang songs of unity and faith, demonstrating to America that during a time of crisis, political differences could be set aside for America's benefit and progress — for the greater good. For a time, political labels were discarded; Americans replaced political party affiliation with nonpartisan behavior. National progress became primary. But sadly, warm, civil feelings disappeared too soon as public officials retreated to their respective "corners" only to fight on in uncivil ways. Incivility's nature says to others: "I'm right and you're wrong, so I won't even listen to you."

"I disapprove of what you say, but I will defend to the death your right to say it," wrote twentieth-century English author Beatrice Evelyn Hall. It is a sentiment echoed by America's founding fathers, but one that is shared by too few of our leaders and citizens today. Incivility must change if America is ever to not only be progressive, but good — worthy of its reputation for greatness in the world.

The Constitution doesn't implore Americans to choose one expression of patriotism over another. Protesting and exercising free-speech rights are both expressions of patriotism, but citizens should express their feelings of patriotism no matter what, while respecting the national anthem and saluting the American flag. Men and women have died to protect everything that the American flag and national anthem represent. Even though protesting and exercising free-speech rights don't always include the expression of good judgment, they're still patriotic actions and can be included in the definition of patriotism.

Defining civics and patriotism also entails an appreciation of American history and gratitude to those who fought for American liberty so that future generations could be free. Ask or read about someone who has lived under a tyrannical regime to learn what it's like to experience freedom: the answer will give all Americans a better patriotic perspective.

The 2016 election of Donald Trump as president of the United States signaled a change in American culture away from tradition and more toward unconventionality. Trump's references to "cleaning DC of the swamp" and getting rid of experienced individuals in DC were a focus of his 2016 campaign. It remains to be seen whether Americans embrace or reject such change. Younger generations in particular don't much care for the drama of incivility and unconventionality. Some individuals have even gone so far as to abandon their political affiliations and political roots in favor of people who exhibit more-dignified bipartisan and nonconfrontational behavior.

A prominent Spokane trial lawyer, a staunch Republican, disliked Trump so much he even wore a Hillary Clinton button on election night 2016. One prominent member of Congress has frustratingly exclaimed, "One day the president is focused on one issue while Congress is focused on another. The next day, the roles are reversed — early in the administration, there has been little legislative coordination between the legislative and executive branches, even though they're of the same political party."

In Greece, Plato, Socrates, and Aristotle laid the foundation for Western philosophy. Plato became entangled in the politics of the city of Syracuse and established a school of higher learning of Western civilization. In 380 BC, Plato wrote "The Republic," a Socratic dialogue that defined justice and commented on the character of the city-state and its relationship to mankind. It remains a classic work of philosophy and helps readers understand the genesis of civic learning since it also includes the study of various forms of government and the design of electoral systems.

Patriotism, then, is fundamentally one's attachment to the country of one's citizenship — we feel connected to our country of birth. It also includes the obligation to know one's country and its history. Being patriotic means being civil and civically knowledgeable. Being civil to others and learning from them is an obligation of patriotism and citizenship. Who knows? Learning from others might even be life changing.

CHAPTER 2

# THE ELEMENTS OF PATRIOTISM

*"The essence of patriotism is the sacrifice of personal interest to public welfare."*
–William H. Burnham

National values are reflected in patriotic feelings, according to Gonzaga University President Thayne McCullouh of Spokane, Washington. McCullouh, GU president since 2010 and before that a campus fixture, believes that values such as hard work for economic success are a product of capitalistic thinking. Bob Smith, a 2016 graduate of Harvard University from an upper-middle-income family, believes that patriotism reflects a person's values — how he or she was raised. If certain values are taught to children — love of country and fair treatment for all, regardless of economic status — then those values become standards for one's patriotism.

Fair play and generosity are American values vividly illustrated in the Marshall Plan adopted after World War II. America, fresh from victory, lent money and assistance to European nations, including Germany, to rebuild.[15] The victors (the Allies) assisted the vanquished (the Axis countries — Germany, Italy, and Japan). George C. Marshall was the architect of the plan (formally called the Foreign Assistance Act of 1948). As Army chief of staff (1939-1945, special envoy to China (1945-1947), secretary of state (1947-1949), and secretary of defense (1950-1951), Marshall was a statesman who answered the call to American service.[16] The plan's moral standard affirmed a national American value of respect for defeated foreign nations in spite of their prior aggression against us. When the United States has helped rebuild foreign countries after wartime victories, we've exercised a moral choice to assist the downtrodden anywhere in the world, a national value that has defined our country.

But Americans have always been on call to other nations experiencing tragedy. Kindness and heartfelt sympathy by Americans accompanied twenty-first-century terrorist tragedies in Europe, where terrorists struck indiscriminately against innocents in Paris, London, and Amsterdam, among others. Americans donate generously to other nations, such as Bosnia and, at times, Cuba, when natural disasters strike their land. Former political opponents President George H. W. Bush and President Bill Clinton even worked side by side to help in the aftermath of a devastating earthquake throughout Haiti in 2010. Though such actions are not uniquely American, US citizens have historically shown a heart for the less fortunate.

*For the Love of Independence and Liberty*

Defining traits of the American character, love of independence and liberty, can be traced back almost four centuries to America's first European settlers. The pilgrims, who set sail on the *Mayflower* in 1620 for the New World, were united in their pursuit of freedom from the religious persecution of England's King James I and the Church of England. The establishment of any new nation necessitated the development of national principles, a compass for the future. Few of the world's nations, however, have had founding principles that have survived basically unchanged throughout history.

But patriots of America (all fifty-six signers of the Declaration of Independence) personally invested in their country's past, present, and future. They (the founding fathers, including Washington, Adams, Jefferson, Hamilton, Jay, and Madison, as well as those who signed the Declaration) sustained victories over internal problems and external threats; from those problems and threats, national values were forged. Shared national values and those revered by all are the lifeblood of patriotism. Reflected glory individually and collectively bolsters a nation's pride and self-worth. Accordingly, Americans have celebrated heroes of history from Paul Revere to John Glenn to Jesse Owens to Martin Luther King, Jr.

The celebration of people and events of accomplishment and great moral strength affirms national values and evokes patriotic emotion — and action. It's why ticker-tape parades down New York's Fifth Avenue occurred and victory gardens were planted during World War II. It's why young men, including future presidents, lined up as eager volunteers to join their country's military after Pearl Harbor was attacked.[17] They wanted to do their patriotic duty by serving their country in time of need. That patriotism continued after the 9/11 attacks in New York, Virginia, and Pennsylvania.

The Olympic Games stand as exhibit number one of the enduring power of patriotism, including love of independence and liberty, across the globe. Humans who attend the Olympic Games from some two hundred countries cheer wildly for athletes from their countries, wave their countries' flags, chant local cheers, and sing national anthems. In the US, ardent fans cheer on their home sports teams as a show of support — a local form of patriotism. But simply cheering every four years for athletes from your own country without an understanding and appreciation of culture, history, values, and character is a hollow form of patriotism. Civic knowledge and vibrant patriotism demand more.

We need leaders who are steeped in the history and values of

America — values such as capitalism, a strong enough American military to protect citizens, low national debt, and an understanding of how government works, among others — but we need a knowledgeable and informed citizenry as well.

Leaders with a strong civics foundation exercise authority based on historical fundamentals that have been tried and proven. Leaders with such experience and knowledge attract followers. Citizens familiar with current events and knowledgeable about basic historical facts are who policy makers expect to populate elective office in America. Voters and citizens likewise respect leaders who are qualified by their track records, deep understanding of issues, and broad perspectives — including the ability to present a national vision and lead others toward it.

Charles is an Uber driver in Spokane, Washington. He sports a gray-haired ponytail and rightfully brags about his forty-five-year marriage, numerous children and grandchildren, and a few great-grandchildren. He speaks proudly of having grown up in a patriotic household and reminisces on times he accompanied his father to public places, including baseball games and airports. He speaks of how his father, a patriotic citizen during WWII, being so proud of men in military uniform, would slip each soldier a "fin" (a five-dollar bill) anonymously wherever he saw them, just to acknowledge the soldiers' attention to duty, to country, and to the cause of freedom. Charles has replicated his deceased father's practice, setting an example for his own relatives and peers.

Likewise, Tim Welsh is a successful Spokane building contractor, a former Army captain in Vietnam, and a person who expresses his charitable nature and patriotic spirit. Having had financial success with his company, Tim has made it a practice to quietly help others — particularly children. He's committed to the American military, drawing on his own national service, and is respectful of those who have served. He and his co-partner routinely help young people learn. For years, Tim has held periodic staff meetings at which he and his co-owners quiz their employees about current affairs, helping them become more informed citizens.

When the United States helped rebuild foreign countries after wartime victories, it exercised a moral choice to assist the downtrodden anywhere in the world, a national value that has defined the United States. The Marshall Plan demonstrated the American standard of helping former enemies ravaged by war. The Marshall Plan's moral standard affirmed a national American value of respect for defeated foreign nations in spite of their prior aggression against the United States. The US provided aid to Korea and Vietnam after conflicts there, and aids Iraq[18] and Afghanistan[19] today. National values undergirded by high moral standards make the United States unique and bolster our sense of patriotism. They are lasting evidence of a country's principles. They provide a glimpse into a nation's soul.

History also teaches a nation's leaders what not to do and how to refrain from making policy mistakes, thereby providing an indirect moral lesson for future conduct. As the Afghanistan and Iraq conflicts escalated, critics referred regularly to the lessons not learned from the Vietnam War as they urged caution in entering wars a far distance from the US.

Such lessons add to the refinement of our national values and help us understand how national values are developed. George Washington long ago warned against American interference in foreign affairs. The Monroe Doctrine, the signature declaration by President James Monroe in 1823, broadly stood for the proposition that if European nations didn't settle in the Western Hemisphere and pose a military threat to the US, America would refrain from European entanglements. The Monroe Doctrine has stood tall as US policy and a respected national value ever since. More than fifty years ago, it was reflected in President John F. Kennedy's directive to the former USSR to stand down on missile placement in Cuba, so close to American soil.

## *National Monuments*

The Statue of Liberty officially celebrated her one-hundredth anniversary in 1986. She rests in New York Harbor as a symbol to foreigners that America is a land that welcomes immigrants. For millions who have immigrated to the States since the late 1800s, the Statue of Liberty has beckoned as an icon of freedom. She represents American acceptance of immigrant relocation to a new land with an opportunity for a better life. Welcoming immigrants to America is a national value that has lasted for more than a century. The Statue of Liberty has always engendered patriotic feelings in immigrants, but also for those born on American soil who acknowledge it as a truly American symbol of the richness, and importance, of social diversity.

Four million people visit the Statue of Liberty National Monument and Ellis Island each year. They do so because the monuments are important to America's history and tell part of America's story. Today, at Ellis Island, descendants of immigrants search historical records for the story of their immigrant ancestors' entry to America. They do so with pride and thanksgiving. Ellis Island links generations and affirms immigrant pride. Singer Neil Diamond's "Coming to America" became a dynamic hit song in 1981 with a positive theme of the history of immigration to the United States. Diamond sang the song at the centennial rededication of the Statue of Liberty in 1986 and again after the attacks of 9/11, then substituting the patriotic lyrics "stand up for America" for "they're comin' to America."

Washington, DC-area war memorials boast the most tourist visits in the United States each year; more than four million people annually visit the Korean War Memorial, the World War II Memorial, Arlington Cemetery, and the Vietnam War Memorial. They are respected sites that evoke recollections of wars fought and sacrifices made. It is impossible for Americans not to recall history when reflecting on these important national monuments; they evoke deep patriotic feelings. American values are reflected in the monuments' inscriptions — and in the monuments themselves. They stand for the sacrifices of past generations for principles of freedom. An understanding of the history of American wars and an appreciation for the ultimate consequences of war are gleaned from visits to war memorials.

The Arlington National Cemetery's website highlights the words "Honor, Remember, Explore." The National World War II Memorial is defined as "a monument to the spirit, sacrifice, and commitment to the American people." At the memorial's dedication in 2004, President George W. Bush declared World War II as a time when Americans "defended our ideals" and that "we began to see that America is stronger when those ideals are fully implemented." He continued to say that "the advances for justice in post-war America made us a better country."[20] Walk by the Vietnam War Memorial in DC to see friends and loved ones shedding tears in memory of the young people memorialized there.

Visitors to the imposing Lincoln Memorial are reminded of how one man's courage and eloquence led a nation to heal the wounds of a bloody civil war, America's deadliest. They also see the exact place from which another man of courage, Dr. Martin Luther King, Jr., delivered his famous "I Have a Dream" speech in 1968. Visitors take away a lasting memory of two men who used the power of patriotic words to lead their nation to higher national values in a time of struggle. Such visits impact and inspire a nation and its citizens.

The Iwo Jima Memorial (the Marine Corps Memorial) in Arlington, Virginia, was designed by sculptor Felix de Weldon and unveiled in 1954.[21] It contains two inscriptions: "In honor and memory of the men of the United States Marine Corps who have given their lives to their country since 10 November 1775" and "Uncommon Valor Was a Common Virtue." This memorial signifies the courage of six Iwo Jima flag raisers on Mt. Suribachi on the island of Iwo Jima, Japan, during World War II. It is an immortal image symbolizing American patriotism and valor. As soldiers from World War II returned alive from war-torn foreign lands, many did so quietly and modestly as examples of "the best of small-town values."

## *The Flag*

In 1916, President Woodrow Wilson issued a proclamation calling for a nationwide observance of Flag Day. It didn't become official until August 1949, when President Harry Truman signed the authorizing legislation. June 14 was then ceremonially proclaimed Flag Day, a day that calls on all Americans to reflect on the foundations of national freedom. National freedom is an American value that is represented by the simple act of flying, or otherwise displaying, our national flag. It's an expression of patriotism that has been embraced by leaders for over two centuries of American history.

While the American flag has changed designs over the centuries, the fifty stars represent the fifty states, and the thirteen stripes represent the original thirteen American colonies — a symbol of our national history. The flag is synonymous with freedom and the struggle for US independence. Flags help define who we are as a nation. To most Americans, they're a symbol of national pride. In 2011, a Pew study found that 75 percent of all Americans display an

American flag at home or at work.[22] Flying the flag is a well-practiced tradition and expression of personal patriotism and love of country.

### *Patriotic Imagery*

There are other tangible symbols of patriotism throughout American history. They call on us to remember and reflect on our national roots. They help define our nation and, in turn, define our feelings about our nationality. Startling images of the attacks of 9/11 remind us of the vulnerability of a free society in a dangerous world, a world of deadly weapons and foreign enemies of our modern United States.

George Washington's crossing of the Delaware River during the American Revolutionary War, depicted in Emanuel Leutze's famous painting,[23] reminds us of the bravery of Washington and the courage of the men under his command. In their threadbare condition as a rag-tag army in icy winter conditions, they surprise attacked Hessian forces in Trenton, New Jersey, on December 26, 1776.[24] That effort followed the publication by reputed founding father Thomas Paine titled "The American Crisis," in which he coined the famous passage:

"These are the times that try men's souls; the summer soldier and the sunshine patriot will, in this crisis, shrink from the service of his country; but he that stands it now, deserves the love and thanks of man and woman. Tyranny, like hell, is not easily conquered; yet we have this consolation with us, that the harder the conflict, the more glorious the triumph."[25]

After Washington ordered the passage read to his troops, it was a morale booster. Today, the quote may not be easily recalled, but the message is clear: in times of struggle, Americans expect triumph, a message that has application throughout America's struggles, growth, and glorious victories — for freedom — for over two centuries. In the case of a national threat, the message underscores the American value of determination.

Collectively, these images and national actions define the American spirit. They provide a basis for patriotic feelings. They undergird our national identity. They permit us the freedom to support our country's aims in the world, but they also free us to boldly seek an unconventional and daring path for our nation.

When the Vietnam War became unpopular, those who deeply opposed the war effort called national leaders to task, using the freedoms of speech and assembly secured for generations to oppose official acts of the government. In doing so, they perpetuated the focus of American heritage on the freedoms that the American system provides. When Americans marched for women's suffrage, opposed the Eighteenth Amendment to the Constitution (Prohibition) and then supported its repeal (Twenty-first Amendment), objected loudly enough that President Richard Nixon resigned from office for official misdeeds, rose up against bigotry and discrimination for civil rights, and when Congress impeached President Clinton, Americans showed their patriotic, wholly American spirit for justice and people-driven national welfare.

Establishing American values has taken generations to perfect. Each generation provides enlightened definitions of patriotism, but they start with the creation of the United States more than two centuries ago when the founding founders embraced the concepts and national values of independence and liberty. National values unite a citizenry — they serve to highlight our common existence. In America's case, they are broad enough to embrace differing points of view.

Independence can mean freedom from rule outside America (i.e., no country other than America can rule her citizens), but it can also mean freedom to challenge oppressive tendencies from within a society. Senator Hubert Humphrey once said, "What we need are critical lovers of America — patriots who express faith in their country by working to improve it."[26] President Woodrow Wilson said, "Sometimes people call me an idealist. Well, that is why I know I am an American. America is the only idealistic nation in the world." Whether idealists or critics, Americans have long identified themselves by those with whom they associate — through images, mottoes, slogans, groups, or names. In doing so, they adopt the values of their national, state, or local associates.

## Mottoes

In 1782, an act of Congress saw the motto "e pluribus unum" adopted for the United States of America. It means "out of many, one." Then President Dwight D. Eisenhower signed a law in 1956 cementing "In God We Trust" as the nation's official motto.[27] Because these mottoes are found on our nation's money, most Americans accept them as representing a collective people, unified under their meanings.

States also have mottoes and symbols that engender patriotic feelings and identification, such as Alaska's "North to the Future," Delaware's "Liberty and Independence," Louisiana's "Union, Justice, and Confidence," and Wyoming's "Equal Rights." Seven states or territories have mottoes that mention God. Illinois's motto is "State Sovereignty, National Unity." New Hampshire's is "Live Free or Die." Wisconsin declares, "Forward." Missouri is the "Show Me State." Washington is the "Evergreen State" and Texas calls itself the "Lone Star State."[28]

States, like America as a whole, have nicknames and mottoes that bind us together as citizens, provide us with a source of identity, and define our values and, ultimately, us. Most Alaskans take pride in their nickname "The Last Frontier" because to them, it is — a land so vast and rich with resources and openness that many who reside there take on the frontier spirit of which they speak and by which they identify themselves.

Purdue University President Mitch Daniels repeatedly referred in his State of the State addresses to the welfare of "Hoosiers," a modern word of endearment for those who reside there. It refers to Indiana's inhabitants as "the bravest, most intelligent, most enterprising, most magnanimous and most democratic of the Great West." What resident of Indiana, therefore, wouldn't want to identify with the word "Hoosier"? Texans also have special self-respect — "Don't Mess with Texas" is a familiar refrain and an original motto, a bumper sticker slogan that first appeared in 1985. Massachusetts's license plates define the state as "The Spirit of America."

These mottoes, slogans, and nicknames help provide us with a collective identity that is the glue that binds us to national and local values.

## *Quotes*

Leaders help us define ourselves, too. President Ronald Reagan's 1981 inaugural address, calling on all Americans to exercise their best patriotic spirit, concluded with these words: "The crisis [high interest rates and a stifling economy] we are facing today . . . does require, however, our best effort and our willingness to believe in ourselves and to believe in our capacity to perform great deeds, to believe that together with God's help we can and will resolve the problems which now confront us. And after all, why shouldn't we believe that? We are Americans."[29]

Statements like these from our leaders bolster our self-identity and cement our idealism.

So, it's easy to understand why American culture has its unique characteristics and why Americans are so proud of our heritage — our history defines and sets out values that we know as patriotic values. It just so happens that as the American system has grown under the initial twin values of freedom and independence, the United States has grown to reflect those values economically, socially, and governmentally. America's independent nature has allowed us to evolve from a discriminatory nation oppressing minorities to a nation cognizant of such shortcomings that provides an internal mechanism — freedom — for adjusting and repairing them.

*Speeches*

Patriotic speeches are often given by public figures, usually office holders and elected officials. They're deemed patriotic because they often render a call to arms, a commitment to freedom, or another statement of national purpose. They're memorable because they often inspire us, call us to commit to our country or our sense of national duty, or affirm national values. Some military officers have delivered memorable remarks inspiring officers to action and calling on others to show their spirit. They must be discussed in the context of patriotism, because they are words of wisdom — words that engender patriotic feelings. They are also words of sacrifice and putting oneself at risk. We call on these remarks periodically to inspire others and to reaffirm what has made America a shining city upon a hill.

Here are a few of many noteworthy patriotic speeches:

1. America's first president, George Washington, was a military general of regal upbringing, respected by all, and was one who carried himself in a dignified way. Called to

serve as president by popular demand, Washington refused to take a salary, instead committing himself to America out of a sense of duty. His Farewell Address (he refused another term as president) is known for its patriotic spirit. Likely written by Washington himself, with help from Madison and Hamilton, his address summarized his eight years of service as president and marked him as a statesman who cared more for America than for his own career. After leaving office, he returned to life as a gentleman farmer at his beloved Mt. Vernon, Virginia, estate, where he and his wife, Mary, are buried. In his farewell, he spoke these words: "Citizens by birth or choice of a common country, that country has a right to concentrate your affections. The name of American, which belongs to you, in your national capacity, must always exalt the just pride of patriotism, more than any appellation derived from local discriminations."[30]

2. In March 1775, Patrick Henry, a patriot referred to as a founding father, gave a stirring speech to the Virginia delegates at the Second Virginia Convention that would go down in history as one of the greatest patriotic speeches of all time. An attorney, orator, and governor of Virginia who served in the Continental Congress, Henry declared his commitment to liberty, saying in that speech, "But as for me, give me liberty or give me death."[31] It was a declaration that would define America's movement to independence. Fearing a strong central government, he opposed ratification of the Constitution, even declining a seat at the Constitutional Convention. He died in 1799[32] after having returned to his law practice.

3. Abraham Lincoln was America's sixteenth president. A self-taught lawyer and statesman, he was assassinated after the conclusion of America's bloodiest war, the Civil War,

which divided America. Lincoln healed the United States, holding the Union together in spite of the secession of eleven Southern states. In 1863, Lincoln delivered his most patriotic speech, the Gettysburg Address, in Gettysburg, Pennsylvania,[33] reportedly after scribbling notes for the speech on the back of an envelope during his train ride to the former battlefield. The speech writing was later disputed. One of the finest oratorical remarks in history, the speech of only 272 words seeks to give meaning to the battle waged there and the American lives lost. It reads, in part, "It is rather for us to be here dedicated to the great task remaining before us — that from these honored dead we take increased devotion to that cause for which they gave the last full measure of devotion — that we here highly resolve that these dead shall not have died in vain — that this nation, under God, shall have a new birth of freedom — and that government of the people, by the people, for the people, shall not perish from the earth." Lincoln's words were carved into a stone cella (a writing on a wall of an ancient temple) on the south wall of the Lincoln Memorial.[34]

4. On March 20, 1912, President Theodore Roosevelt, a gifted orator, writer, and explorer who was America's twenty-sixth president (from 1901 to 1909[35]), delivered a patriotic speech in Carnegie Hall in New York City, declaring the right of the people to rule — a fundamental tenet of democracy. Roosevelt stressed the importance of a civically knowledgeable populace able to govern itself, while a civically ignorant people cannot. An anarchist, upset that Roosevelt was seeking a third term as president, shot Roosevelt, but Roosevelt still gave the speech — even though the assassin's bullet penetrated the written speech in Roosevelt's chest pocket. He told the crowd that he'd been

shot and referred to himself as a "bull moose." He was ultimately unsuccessful in his bid for a third term.[36] Roosevelt said: "The great fundamental issue now before the Republican Party and before our people can be stated briefly. It is: Are the American people fit to govern themselves? I believe they are."

5. Franklin Delano Roosevelt was the only president to be elected four consecutive times.[37] He entered the presidency during America's Great Depression, a time when the economy struggled and Americans suffered widespread unemployment. Considered a savior by many, Roosevelt ushered in a series of government programs and public works projects, some of which have lasted to this day (Social Security, for instance). In 1933, he delivered his inaugural address, in which he said, "This is preeminently the time to speak the truth, the whole truth, frankly and boldly. Nor need we shrink from honestly facing conditions in our country today. This great nation will endure, as it has endured, will revive and will prosper. So, first of all, let me assert my firm belief that the only thing we have to fear is fear itself — nameless, unreasoning, unjustified terror, which paralyses needed efforts to convert retreat into advance."[38] His speech was designed to reassure Americans that they and their government together would overcome the depression's devastation.

Roosevelt, a former New York governor and assistant secretary of the US Navy, again recognized the public's need for inspiration when he delivered an address after the Japanese attacked Pearl Harbor in Oahu, Hawaii, in December of 1941: "With confidence in our armed forces, with the unbounding determination of our people, we will gain the inevitable triumph, so help us God."[39] Roosevelt died in office in 1945.

6. In his 1962 inaugural address, President John F. Kennedy delivered two famous lines that have often been quoted as extremely patriotic sentiments in the history of such speeches. "And so, my fellow Americans, ask not what your country can do for you, ask what you can do for your country. My fellow citizens of the world, ask not what America will do for you, but what we can do together for the freedom of man."[40] President Kennedy was promiscuous, but by today's standards, he was a more conservative president than other modern Democratic presidents with a liberal philosophy. He favored a strong military and broad tax relief. Having narrowly defeated Richard Nixon in the 1960 election, Kennedy went on to fight the former Soviet Union over missiles in Cuba, and he supported a strong civil rights agenda that was enacted after he was assassinated in 1963.[41] After Kennedy was assassinated, his successor, Lyndon B. Johnson, passed major civil rights laws and credited Kennedy. Kennedy backed up his call to Americans for selfless duty to country and the freedom of man in 1961.[42]

7. On May 12, 1962, Army General Douglas MacArthur delivered a patriotic speech to military cadets at his alma mater, West Point, the US Army's military academy in New York. MacArthur was a military man through and through, a five-star general who grew up in a military family, became Army chief of staff, and had a confrontation with President Harry Truman over MacArthur's desire to invade China in 1951.[43] It led to MacArthur's firing. His speech to West Point cadets is renowned for its patriotic spirit and admonition to military personnel, saying, "Yours is the profession of arms, the will to win, the sure knowledge that in war, there is no substitute for victory; that if you lose, the nation will be destroyed;

that the very obsession of your public service must be: Duty, Honor, Country."[44] Those hallowed words reverently dictate what soldiers ought to be, what they can be, and what they will be. MacArthur died in 1964.[45]

8. Martin Luther King, Jr., was a Baptist pastor, a political activist, and a leader of the national civil rights movement. He preached nonviolence and civil disobedience, though violence periodically accompanied the civil rights movement. In 1968, he delivered a patriotic speech from the steps of the Lincoln Memorial, his "I Have a Dream" speech, saying in part, "When the architects of our republic wrote the magnificent words of the Constitution and the Declaration of Independence, they were signing a promissory note to which every American was to fall heir. This note was a promise that all men — yes, Black men as well as white men — would be guaranteed the unalienable rights of life, liberty, and the pursuit of happiness . . . I still have a dream. It is a dream deeply rooted in the American dream. I have a dream that one day this nation will rise up, live out the true meaning of its creed: We hold these truths to be self-evident, that all men are created equal."[46]

Dr. King ended his stirring speech by saying, "When we allow freedom to ring, we will be able to speed up that day, join hands and sing 'Free at last, Free at last, Thank God almighty we are free at last.'" King later died a violent death in 1968 at the hands of an assassin, James Earl Ray.[47]

9. Ronald Reagan was America's fortieth president, known for having ushered in a new era of challenging the size and scope of government. Many admired his principled stance on politics, even though the size of government increased during his two terms. A gifted orator with a Hollywood acting career background, Reagan summed up his philosophy of government in his 1989 farewell address,

saying, "As long as we remember our first principles and believe in ourselves, the future will be ours. And something else we learned: Once you begin a great movement, there's no telling where it will end. We meant to change a nation, and instead, we changed a world."[48]

Reagan expressed his feelings about government when he said, "The most terrifying words in the English language are: I'm from the government and I'm here to help." And, "Government's view of the economy could be summed up in a few short phrases: If it moves, tax it. If it keeps moving, regulate it. And if it stops moving, subsidize it."[49] He died of Alzheimer's disease in 2004.

### Citizen Action

War and peace, and whether and how to aid other nations, have been topics of American debate and discussion throughout US history. After America attained its own freedom and grew economically, it exported that freedom by assisting other nations striving to be free.

Some of the efforts have drawn universal praise — World Wars I and II, for instance. Others remain steeped in controversy. American intervention in Vietnam in the 1960s, leading to war, resulted in years of national upheaval, spurred by the protests of millions of young people.

The anti-war movement aided the government's decision to withdraw troops.[50] The trauma of the time left deep scars but also serves as inspiration that the American people can have a say in how they are governed.

The American tradition of citizen protest was not deterred by the federal government's attempts to subdue it in the 1960s and early 1970s, and a significant change in American policy resulted. Such is the hallmark of a free and open society, where the national government does not or cannot oppress disagreement. We are witnessing a similar debate and pattern today with the discussions about gun laws and health insurance.

Similarly, the anti-Trump movement that developed after 2016 has evolved passionately but peacefully. Protest is part of the American fabric and is largely a consequence of America's devotion to freedom. American voters after national elections have largely accept the outcome, with the exception of the 2020 election, when violence broke out at the Capitol on January 6, 2021. As of this writing, the violence has not been duplicated, perhaps in part because the court system has refused to extend Constitutional protection to such behaviors. The First Amendment protects speech, not violent action.

The American model for citizen input started with the Boston Tea Party in 1776, the spirit of which has in recent years been reflected in the Occupy and Tea Party efforts. In 2012, the anti-gun and resistance movements, all in the name of philosophical differences and what's good for America, and all in a free society, received national support primarily from communities that suffered from gun violence. It makes the United States unique — and special.

The same freedoms, born of national values, do not exist in many countries around the world, including China, Russia, and Venezuela. According to a 2016 report by Freedom House[51] on global political and civil rights, more than half of the 195 countries surveyed were deemed only partly free or not free.

Americans who don't realize how foreign policy can be changed by public outcry, or how other public policy decisions can be influenced, are weaker citizens for their ignorance. Those who don't exercise their precious right to vote sacrifice the opportunity to shape their nation, state, or community.

In 2016, only about 55 percent of voting-age citizens bothered to vote — the lowest turnout since 1996.[52] Instead, they let others choose for them, nullifying an important aspect of their citizenship. In an age of ubiquitous communications, passive citizenship leads to unwise public policies. More than two-thirds of Americans polled by Politico/Morning Consult said they favored stricter gun control laws.[53] Yet, Congress has done little in response. If citizens don't understand the American justice system, they're at its mercy. And if leaders don't know how history treated an issue, they may be destined to repeat a failure. There is abundant criticism of the wars in Iraq and Afghanistan, particularly from antiwar activists, comparing these wars to Vietnam. Many crime-convicted citizens have questioned their legal representation and have been set free by new evidence.

The Declaration of Independence sets forth "unalienable rights," and the Constitution enumerates the Bill of Rights. Those who are ignorant of their rights, rights that have survived for over two hundred years, are not fully engaged in the life of America; they're unable to fully feel the patriotism and national values that bind a society. A nation whose inhabitants are ignorant of their country's history, economics, foreign policy, and government will eventually suffer consequences for that disengagement. They'll be lesser citizens, ignorant of the benefits and responsibilities of citizenship. They'll also be passive contributors to America's eventual demise, since many have called for big economic changes in America (e.g., Medicare for all and free college tuition) that could lead to financial peril. If American citizens want to be fully alive to the country's true identity, they must actively participate.

One could make a persuasive argument that this is precisely what is happening in the United States now. US credibility has been eroded by criticism from America's national media as watchdogs of government, and Congress is continually criticized. Many citizens are not watching, don't understand, or don't care. Public officials, if they're inclined, are therefore able to take actions that could harm many Americans by adopting punitive taxes or oppressive regulations.

Washington, DC, is a mass of insiders who won't share their deepest thoughts with the public. That's why citizen engagement is so important. Even though patriotism is an amalgam of many values, mottoes, and words, it is a concept subject to various interpretations.

Patriotism's elements may not be subject to universal definition; the word generally includes three elements: love of country, sacrifice for country, and commitment to country. Patriotism is primarily country oriented. It is strongly associated with war, because serving one's country in wartime or conflict is itself considered an act of patriotism. Patriotism also includes death for one's country: in the line of duty, it's considered the "ultimate sacrifice for patriotism." However, patriotism is not required to always be positive; it's possible for Americans to criticize their country but still be considered patriotic. Many times in American history, Americans have stood against their country, arguing a course of action they believed would improve the nation. The strong, conflicted feelings about the American Civil War, the civil rights movement of the 1960s, and opposing views about American entry into other wars (WWI, WWII, and Vietnam, for example) chronicle situations that divided Americans as partisans with differing points of view about government commitments.

A free society has room for differing views and different patriotic stances. But other expressions of patriotism have appeared throughout American history. The National Museum of Patriotism, now a virtual museum and recently referred to as the National Foundation of Patriotism, is based in Atlanta, Georgia. Its founder and chairman is Nicholas D. Snider. The museum's home page states, "The National Museum of Patriotism is an inspiration to all who embrace life, liberty and the pursuit of happiness promised us by our founding fathers."

Snider believes that many Americans are concerned about where the next generation will learn what it means to be an American, and that's why he created this privately sponsored museum. Though the physical museum is now closed, it has been a modern example of nationalism denied commercial success. It followed the closure of another exhibit that extolled the virtue of a free-enterprise economy in Oklahoma City, Oklahoma. Its collection of patriotic themes, music, poetry, odes to America's patriotic past, and extensive references to American flags has become less commercially attractive during national economic hardship.

But their current form exemplifies patriotism and reminds Americans of their patriotic past. When Americans are asked about their patriotism, they generally consider how much they love their country, how happy they are to be Americans, and how fairly they feel treated in their daily lives living in the States. And Americans are especially patriotic around inherently patriotic holidays, such as Independence Day, Memorial Day, and President's Day.

There is also a generational divide over whether Americans believe the US is "exceptional." Only 32 percent of millennial-age respondents surveyed (eighteen to twenty-nine) believe so, while 64 percent of those age sixty-four or over believe the US is "the greatest country in the world." With some exceptions, the older the American, the greater their patriotism. On a "love of country" scale alone, from 2003 to 2010, one poll showed that 91 percent of Americans aged sixty-four or older considered themselves to be "very patriotic," while only 70 percent of younger people did, which is still a relatively high number.[54] There are also separations demographically between Republicans and Democrats: in 2010, Gallup found that 52 percent of Republicans and 20 percent of Democrats considered themselves "extremely patriotic."[55]

A 2011 poll by Pew Research found that 91 percent of Americans believed our nation's success was due to freedom, 85 percent believed our national work ethic was responsible for national success, and 82 percent credited our natural resources as the reason. Military strength, democratic government, and the free market economy registered percentages in the seventies, and 63 percent credited religious faith and values. Fifty-eight percent credited racial and ethnic makeup as the reasons for American success.[56]

What these surveys show is that younger Americans are largely below the levels of patriotism felt by older Americans where love of country is concerned. If younger Americans are describing themselves as less patriotic, then the civics teaching deficits of the past may be catching up with them, making it more necessary than ever for the United States government to commit to reinstating civic learning in our classrooms. Doing so will produce a generation of civically minded individuals with enhanced patriotic feelings who, in turn, recognizing the importance of civic literacy and its effect on American culture, may pass on such feelings to their children. If, however, the millennial generation, which has been shortchanged on civic learning, fails to "catch up," it will be consequential to American society and the perpetuation of the American system of representative government and democracy as it has been known for over two hundred years.

Patriotic feelings are also engendered by individuals' sacrifices for their country and may explain the gap between younger and older Americans' perceptions. Older Americans are more likely to have served in the military than those younger.[14] The character of military service also has an impact on patriotism. Those who served in World

War II had different wartime experiences than those who served in Vietnam, Iraq, or Afghanistan. Those at home generally supported WWII, while the other wars had more adamant critics.

The sacrifice of public service, even in elected office, is deemed a commitment to country worthy of respect. Even though federal worker job satisfaction ranked below private-sector employee job satisfaction in 2011, more than six in ten federal employees were satisfied, believing that they were contributing to America's welfare.[58]

Seventy-five percent of all Americans fly the American flag; a 2002 poll[59] showed that 83 percent fly their flags during Independence Day celebrations. Most Americans consider flag flying to be an act of patriotism. Paying taxes is considered patriotic. Singing the national anthem ("The Star-Spangled Banner") is considered patriotic. So is reciting the Pledge of Allegiance.

Acts of commitment to country are more-personal forms of patriotic expression. A recent Harvard University survey[60] showed that a surprising number of millennials preferred volunteering to voting. While it's certainly preferable to vote *and* volunteer, patriotic acts and direct contributions (e.g., tutoring a child or delivering hot meals to shut-ins) are becoming more frequent. Disgusted with politics, some millennials opt for nonpolitical, direct community service contributions; they see community service as an act of patriotism.

There have been few popular patriotic songs written recently; most are written by country singers, and patriotic country songs proliferate. Usually patriotic songs emanate out of a time of conflict or disruption. We know of songs of the Revolutionary War, songs of WWII, songs of the Great Depression, and the protest songs of Vietnam. Popular singer John Mayer recorded a song in 2009, perhaps one of the last popular social commentary songs in America, titled "Waiting on the Word to Change." It was written perhaps for a generation tired of war and expecting a cycle of peace to emerge. The song speaks to the perceived inability of the younger generation to make a change in the world — from conflict to peace — lamenting their lack of power in a system of which they don't feel a part. Mayer suggests that the news is skewed against their interests and that they're at a distance from national power. Rather than being traditionally patriotic, it's a protest song written by one with liberal views implying victimhood.

It seems to pit one generation against another, suggesting that the older generation routinely hides information from the younger. It's polarizing, but the tune is pleasant to hear. While there are other modern songs that may qualify as patriotic, they're not as well known or recognized as songs of the past. Some songs, such as Lonestar's 2001 hit, "I'm Already There," speak of soldiers and the loneliness of war.

J.D. Vance wrote a best-selling book titled *Hillbilly Elegy*. It was an attempt to explain what it's like to grow up poor and what elements of American culture are perpetuated based on social status and exposure. Vance escaped poverty and his cultural background by hard work, educational excellence, and good fortune. President Trump's presidential campaign spoke to a vast population of disaffected Americans for whom the American dream was elusive. Poverty-stricken, hopeless, unconnected to centers of influence, and lacking Vance's ability to succeed, citizens supported the Trump message, clinging to the notion that as a person of wealth, he'd protect them as an advocate, connecting them to possible success through change in the American government. Even though Mrs. Clinton won the popular American vote (but lost the electoral college vote per the Constitution), time will tell if voters misplaced their loyalty, let down by the foregoing elements of patriotism.

CHAPTER 3

# ESSENTIALS OF PATRIOTISM

*"Patriotism is a lively sense
of collective responsibility."*
–Richard Aldington

Before one can confidently utter or advocate for the word patriotism or some variant thereof, one must define the word; that's where patriotism essentials play a part.

The essentials of American patriotism are: (1) American citizenship and the constitutional freedoms it affords; (2) commitment to country and loyalty to the American native land; (3) ideally, a public platform from which to extol the virtues of American freedom; (4) engagement in American life and showing an interest in public policy; (5) caring enough about America to speak up; and (6) respect for authority.

*1. American Citizenship and Freedom*

In order to be an effective and credible spokesperson for patriotism, one must be committed to the United States through some form of citizenship. Naturalization or being a natural citizen (born in the United States) are the best ways, but not the only ones — a foreign national committed to America can effectively speak out on its behalf without attendant citizenship

— but credibility follows citizen status. Fundamentally, patriotism supports freedom, and vice versa.

## 2. *Commitment and Loyalty*

Any spokesperson advocating for American patriotism is more effective if that person's commitment to America is demonstrated, either by actions or by words. Joining the American military or testifying to an example experienced that demonstrates how America has benefitted an individual usually suffices. Both examples show a commitment to one's native land.

## 3. *Public Platform*

Usually celebrities or those in a public position are best able to espouse patriotic essentials. Movie or television stars, elected officials, or those who have notoriety receive the most public attention connected to their patriotic pronouncements. When public officials or celebrities speak lovingly of their country, their followers take note, and many want to replicate such behavior.

## 4. *Engagement*

Those who are engaged in American life, experience the freedoms America offers, and express an interest in the "American way" are the best spokespeople for patriotism. They've experienced, through business or otherwise, tangible benefits of American free enterprise and can speak of what they've learned and how the American system has been of benefit to them.

## 5. Speaking Up

While many Americans treasure their relative anonymity, it takes a special type to speak out about how they've benefitted from their American citizenship or elements of patriotism. Being outspoken about patriotism you've experienced takes courage and draws attention, sometimes unwanted. But, when an American speaks out in support of American values, it's usually refreshing — though sometimes outspokenness can highlight other personal flaws one would rather keep private. Oftentimes, individuals whom the public considers heroic for their patriotic expressions are not heroic in other nonpatriotic instances.

## 6. Respect for Authority

Respect for authority does not mean authority rules — it is more nuanced. Respect for authority means humility, a healthy respect for other people's points of view, and recognition that many "bosses" hold a position over others and others should pay respect to that higher position. It does not mean the authority is always right or is not subject to criticism or suggestions for improvement. Patriotism includes respect for authority as well as self-respect, no matter one's ranking in any organization. Oftentimes, a person without authority has ideas that could benefit the organization. Those ideas should be respected and considered, even if suggested by one not in a position of authority.

Andreas Wimmer, writing in *Foreign Affairs* magazine, has opined that patriotic behavior can have a positive side, while nationalism can be negative.[61] He likens negative nationalism to white supremacy, restrictive immigration policies, and economic protectionism. Patriotism, however, builds national solidarity and benefits many individuals without abundant material goods. Wimmer suggests that national solidarity can transcend many ethnic and regional identities. He also suggests that political representation often breeds national identification — when a minority person holds a public position, that public official attracts those of the same ethnic makeup, and ethnic patriotism increases. Minority entertainers often speak to, and attract, those who identify with that person.

Others see patriotism negatively. Oscar Wilde once said, "Patriotism is the virtue of the vicious." Communist Karl Marx called patriotism a menace to liberty. Samuel Johnson, an English writer and poet, once declared, "Patriotism is the last refuge of a scoundrel." Leo Tolstoy was an ardent antipatriot. Gustave Herve, a French politician and writer, another antipatriot, once called patriotism "a superstition" and "more inhumane than religion."

But such pronouncements don't acknowledge the benefits of patriotism — a national identity that extols virtuous behavior, commitment to a national purpose, and recognition of minority or dissenting points of view. Granted, many minority viewpoints are not made public, but the American system affords dissenters the freedom to speak.

Patriotism is not only for the wealthy or powerful, but it's also unfair to assert that patriotism only exists for the powerful or wealthy. Patriotism and use of the American political system, anchored by the Constitution, are available to those without wealth or inherent power. Again, the Parkland, Florida, tragedy was an event that prompted powerless students to rise up to demand political action. They were successful in the Florida legislature with gun control provisions even though they possessed no inherent wealth or power.

When advocates raised the issue of female voting rights, they were grassroots oriented. Yet, they accomplished their goal of women's suffrage. The same is true for constitutional amendments affecting Prohibition. Americans were able to effect national change without inherent wealth and power. They used the Constitution as their vehicle for societal change.

Some assert that America stands primarily for militarism and that patriotism supports militarism. While that's untrue, it's clear that the American military has an influence on world peace and preventing some countries from oppressing others. President George H. W. Bush coalesced numerous nations when Iraq's Saddam Hussein invaded its neighbor Kuwait. Presidents Wilson and Roosevelt reluctantly entered world wars, but America's presence ultimately ended those international conflicts. Nor is patriotism an excuse for using military might. Rather than using American military might for personal gain, instead it can be argued that military might was used to right a wrong, prevent an invasion by the strong against the weak, or correct abusive action by one country against another, which would have had the effect of oppressing another human's freedom.

Through advances in innovation and technology, America has developed ways to protect its citizens from invasion by foreign governments. Threats to American freedom have existed since 1776, and it is American militarism, expensive though it may be, that has protected and continues to protect all Americans from foreign invasion. While some may argue that militarism is merely "toys" that cause mass deaths, a better argument is that without such military might, America might not exist in a way that allows Americans to practice the freedoms afforded by the Constitution.

In short, American patriotism is essential for freedom — for all. And that freedom is essential for American patriotism. George

Bernard Shaw one said, "Patriotism is, fundamentally, a conviction that a particular country is the best in the world because you were born in it," but American patriotism also must have goodness as part of its reason for being.

America has stood for goodness over its relatively short existence, a goodness born of the freedoms it espouses, especially those in the Constitution.

## CHAPTER 4

# DISSENT IS PATRIOTIC

*"Dissent is the purest form of patriotism."*
–Thomas Jefferson

The quote above is usually attributed to Jefferson,[62] America's third president (1801-1809), who was tall for his time (about six feet, two inches) and was bright and creative (he composed his own version of the Bible). He served as vice president under President John Adams and was minister to France; he was also a landowner and farmer.

An accomplished architect, Jefferson founded and designed the University of Virginia in 1819, and he also designed his residence in Charlottesville, Virginia, called Monticello. Jefferson was the epitome of the Renaissance man, and his interest in religion and philosophy was reflected in his selection as president of the American Philosophical Society.

Dissent has been part of the American experience since before the country was formed in 1776. It's an integral part of the fabric of Americanism, even somewhat expected in a free society. The founding fathers wanted to ensure that liberty included the right to criticize leaders, government actions, and others in positions of authority. Dissent was safeguarded when the founders assured that the Constitution and the Bill of Rights afforded citizens the right of free speech. While speech is not always "free," notably in cases where free speech endangers others (yelling "fire!" in a crowded theater or inciting others to riot), generally Americans can utter whatever they want without fear or expectation of reprisal or being hauled away to jail for speaking their mind.

The United States tolerates actions that in many other countries would likely lead to arrest. For instance, the Supreme Court has held that flag burning or other desecration of the American flag is "speech" and is thus constitutionally protected. That's part of the freedom and liberty accorded us under our Constitution.

As Michael Ratner and Margaret Ratner Kunstler wrote in their 2011 book, *Hell No: Your Right to Dissent in 21st Century America*, "Taken together, the right to free speech, the right of assembly, and the explicit right to express grievances to the government add up to an expansive right to 'dissent' in the Bill of Rights.

"Beyond written or spoken words, the right to dissent is the right of citizens to organize themselves, to associate, to make themselves heard in order to achieve political and social change, and oppose government policies without fear of impediment or reprisal."

There are certainly many instances in history when dissent was considered patriotic, but the following capture a few of the more prominent examples.

*War of American Independence (Revolutionary War)*

Perhaps the most dramatic example of dissent occurred just before the United States was created in 1776. It rivals any dissent since. A band of dissidents stood up to King George of Great Britain, under whose control they had been, to object to taxation by the mother country (England) and other oppressions, as enumerated in the Declaration of Independence. That their patriotism was born of dissent resulted in the United States' crafting a constitution that embraced dissent — a constitution that has lasted longer than any other in history.⁶³ They dissented vocally and through their actions, resulting in a revolutionary war with Great Britain that brought British armies to America to fight against the dissidents.

The revolution and the formation of the United States of America thereafter produced many heroes. George Washington, America's first president, was a battle-tested general of stature and accomplishment. Washington carried himself with dignity and repute as citizens called on him to serve.

John Adams, America's second president, was short in stature but tall in statesmanship, having declared, "Our Constitution was made only for a moral and religious people. It is wholly inadequate to the government of any other."

Long considered the author of the Declaration of Independence, Thomas Jefferson, a scholar of many interests and accomplishments, later became America's third president, responsible for the Lewis and Clark expedition and the Louisiana Purchase.

The American Revolution gathered like-minded "patriots" to its cause: freedom. Other heroic figures stand out, such as the fifty-six men who signed the Declaration of Independence, pledging "their lives, their fortunes, and their sacred honor."⁶⁴

Men such as John Hancock, perhaps possessing the most prominent signature of all who signed; Alexander Hamilton, America's first treasury secretary and one of the authors of the Federalist Papers; Benjamin Franklin, a leading author, politician, and printer, who once said, "An investment in education pays the best interest"; and James Madison, who became America's fourth president, considered by some to be the father of the Constitution and Bill of Rights. Others thought John Marshall, America's fourth Supreme Court Chief Justice, was father of the Constitution because his opinions solidified the Supreme Court as America's third coequal branch of government.[65] A Federalist, Marshall served uninterrupted as chief justice for thirty-five years.

## *The American Civil War*

The dissent of the Southern states led to the American Civil War (1862-1865), the bloodiest war in American history. Eleven states seceded from the Union. Upset by antislavery forces and the economic pressure that resulted, Southerners fought the Union states as President Lincoln fought to preserve the Union. The Civil War claimed the lives of more than six hundred thousand, who died from combat, starvation, disease, and accident.[66]

Battlefields marking America's heritage dot the East — from Washington, DC, to Pennsylvania and from Virginia to South Carolina. The war divided families, with some fighting for their regions (North or South) and some on behalf of their states. War fighting was more primitive then, with some soldiers simply facing their enemies and exchanging gunfire. Modern medical assistance now makes Civil War treatments seem crude and primitive.

President Lincoln's leadership before, during, and after the war led many historians to deem him the country's greatest president ever. After the South was defeated and the Union was maintained, Lincoln, in a gesture intended to unite the South and the North, ordered the White House band to play, "Dixie," the South's battle cry, declaring it "America's song." He was not gloating over the North's victorious efforts, but instead seeking unity and harmony among Americans.

Sadly, Lincoln was assassinated only five days after the war ended, before he could see the eleven Southern states that seceded from the Union return to statehood.[67]

## The Civil Rights Movement

Martin Luther King, Jr., a Baptist pastor, Nobel Peace Prize winner, and orator, was the face of the American civil rights movement. He and his followers dissented from American racist policies, calling for nonviolent protest and civil disobedience as they led others to demand racial equality. King learned from and tried to emulate the style of Indian activist Mahatma Gandhi, who adopted a nonviolent approach to protest and dissent.[68]

King delivered his famous "I Have a Dream" speech on August 28, 1963, at the Lincoln Memorial in Washington, DC, one of several landmarks in the civil rights movement.

The civil rights movement culminated for many in a march in Washington, DC, the same day as King's speech. Though it was hot and humid, some two hundred thousand demonstrators participated, adopting a major campaign of civil resistance that led to civil rights talks and negotiations over a period of years.[69] They lined up on the National Mall between the Lincoln Memorial and the Washington Monument in a show of support for peaceful change. It was an act of patriotism. Working with Congress and state legislatures and numerous government officials led to the passage of the Civil Rights Act of 1964 and the Voting Rights Act of 1965. Later that decade, Blacks rioted in California, Washington, DC, and other cities, protesting continued discrimination and the lack of economic opportunity. Blacks unhappy with national civil rights leadership in these cases turned more militant.

As background, in 1865, Congress passed the Constitution's Thirteenth Amendment, which ended slavery. The Fourteenth Amendment gave African Americans citizenship, and the Fifteenth gave African American males the right to vote. Reconstruction ended in 1876, and Southern whites in office began to clamp down on the voting rights of African American males and poor whites through voter registration requirements that resulted in disenfranchisement.[70] In the late 1800s, Southern states passed so-called Jim Crow laws that mandated segregation in all public facilities, including schools. In 1896, the Supreme Court endorsed the doctrine of separate but equal, despite the fact that facilities such as schools and job opportunities were far from equal.[71]

Institutional discrimination occurred until President Lyndon Johnson, a Southern Democrat and successor to the beloved, assassinated John F. Kennedy, pushed legislation through Congress in Kennedy's memory. The civil rights movement, therefore, represented a continuing dissident movement by American citizens well within their citizenship rights to push their government into equality under the law for all. After the march on Washington in 1963, King and other civil rights leaders met with President Kennedy and Vice President Johnson to discuss legislation to end Jim Crow.

## *The Vietnam War*

The war began in 1955, allegedly because of the Domino Theory, which posited that if Vietnam fell to communism, other Asian countries would do the same.[72] By 1965, many Americans — particularly college students — saw it as an unwinnable war that was taking thousands of American and Vietnamese lives in vain. Ultimately, fifty-eight thousand American soldiers lost their lives [73] and three hundred thousand were wounded, many maimed for life.[74] In 1965, after the US began regular bombings in North Vietnam, and the draft was increased from three thousand monthly to three hundred thousand, marches and sit-ins protesting the war spread across the country. Hundreds of thousands of Americans wanting peace and objecting to a government they saw as duplicitous took to the streets protesting the war effort. Some American young men fled to Canada and other countries to avoid military service, because they didn't believe in the Vietnam War. Some deemed them patriotic; some deemed them traitorous. The demonstrations from Cambridge to Berkeley provided a powerful example of Americans exercising their rights to gather and protest against government action.

The Vietnam War affected four American presidents: Eisenhower, who first sent military "advisors" to Vietnam; Kennedy, who intensified the effort; Johnson, who committed thousands to military service there; and Nixon, who committed troops but finally ended the conflict, declaring that "peace with honor" had been achieved, despite the fact that South Vietnam had fallen to the communist North. The protests, which continued until the war ended in 1974, played a significant role in convincing Nixon to withdraw American troops.[75]

The release of the Pentagon Papers to the *New York Times* in 1971 led many Americans to the conclusion that their government had been dishonest in its persecution of the war, lying about casualties and military campaigns expanded beyond Vietnam.[76] The Vietnam War still makes Americans bristle with contempt for dishonest government leaders, captured by Nixon's never admitting American defeat or vulnerability. But the ultimate success of the massive protests was their power to result in change in the United States.

### Women's Right to Vote

The fight for women's suffrage began in earnest in the 1840s. In 1848, the Seneca Falls Convention, the first women's rights assembly, passed a resolution calling for women to be afforded the right to vote. In 1869, two national suffrage organizations were created — one led by Elizabeth Cady Stanton and Susan B. Anthony, the other by Lucy Stone.[77] The two organizations merged in 1890 as the National American Woman Suffrage Association, and the battle for suffrage began to gain momentum. Anthony was a Quaker and an ardent antislavery advocate. She and Stanton were lifelong friends who were committed to universal suffrage and an end to other-gender discrimination. Though other countries allowed women to vote before America, the women's suffrage movement eventually succeeded on American shores in 1920 by way of the Nineteenth Amendment.

The suffrage movement was also a prominent example of patriotic dissent. Notably, in 1917, hundreds of supporters of the National Woman's Party picketed the White House.[78] They were arrested and sent to prison, where some went on a hunger strike and were subsequently force-fed. Anthony herself was arrested after she and fifteen other women managed to vote in 1872.[79] Anthony was the only one of the sixteen women arrested. She was found guilty and fined, but she was defiant in court, vowing not to pay a cent. She fulfilled that promise, and the enormous publicity her trial received gave new momentum to the suffrage movement.[80]

Women speaking out on political and government matters started much earlier, though. Women such as Abigail Adams played a prominent role, as did her husband (John Adams), battling stereotypes that women should be relegated to raising children and cooking to satisfy their husbands.[81] The women's suffrage movement was broad, however, encompassing women of all economic conditions and racial backgrounds, effectively debunking the notion that women were inferior and were stepping beyond their "natural" status. It's an example of how dissent and perseverance led to a change of American policy. Stanton and Anthony died within four years of each other in the early 1900s.

## Prohibition and Its Repeal

Prohibition and its repeal represent two more examples of how political advocacy by average Americans can lead to policy change at the national level. Prohibition represented an era of outlawing alcohol production, importation, transportation, and sale in America.

The period lasted thirteen years and gave rise to an illicit alcohol trade by unsavory actors (the gangster Al Capone, among others).[82] Through the sheer determination and political dissent by Americans, as well as practical considerations, the policy was changed and the Twenty-first Amendment replaced the Prohibition Amendment. Originally promoted by "dry" advocates (including pious members of Protestant churches and various social progressives) in an attempt to purify American society, the Prohibition movement sought to shut down unsavory saloons and eliminate family struggles, violence, corruption, and alcoholism caused by alcohol consumption.

To many, Prohibition was a moral issue intended to "clean up" American society. It was supported by the Women's Christian Temperance Movement, coordinated by the Anti-Saloon League, and opposed by Catholics and German Lutherans. It was a classic political brawl, with emotions running high on both sides of the issue. The Volstead Act was passed by Congress, thus enabling the Eighteenth Amendment — the amendment that provided for Prohibition.

It wasn't long, though, before the amendment was routinely violated, criminal elements stepped in to sell alcohol, and bootlegging became widespread. A new movement began to reverse the Eighteenth Amendment. Because many states lost tax revenue and urban crime increased, the repeal movement intensified, resulting in the eventual adoption of the Twenty-first Amendment, which reversed Prohibition.

In the aftermath of the repeal effort, for a time alcohol consumption was reduced, temporarily socializing a portion of the American population in temperate habits, but Prohibition was a good example of public policy being caught up in the public push for change and then another push for a change — back to how things were.

## *The 1968 Summer Olympics*

The 1968 Summer Olympic Games were held in October in Mexico City, Mexico, the first Games ever held in a Spanish-speaking country. They were marked by the fist-raising Black Power salute of two Black American Olympic sprinters as they received medals for their victorious running of the 200 meter sprint. It was a form of protest that garnered worldwide attention. Tommie Smith and John Carlos, both tall and gifted athletes who also played professional football, raised black-gloved fists overhead when the American National Anthem was played as they received the gold and bronze medals, respectively.[83]

In his autobiography, Smith said their actions were not a Black Power salute, but rather a human rights salute. Both went on to higher academic pursuits. White Australian Peter Norman, who wore an American civil rights badge to support his podium mates, won the silver medal.

The event caused international turmoil, especially when the International Olympic Committee banned Smith and Carlos from the Olympics for life; Norman was kicked off the Australian Olympic team in 1972.[84] The incident has been compared to the dissent expressed in 2017 by NFL players kneeling during the National Anthem to protest the treatment of Blacks in this country.

### "Black Lives Matter"

This is a slogan coined in 2013 by African Americans to protest the violence, including deadly shootings, by police arresting Blacks across America.[85] "Black Lives Matter" has become a rallying cry for those who feel oppressed in America and those who support them. Some call it a new civil rights movement. Reaction to the slogan has been mixed: many endorse the slogan and the protests by its supporters, while others have responded with slogans such as "All Lives Matter." When presidential candidate Martin O'Malley, the white governor of Maryland, declared that "all lives matter" during the Democratic presidential debate in October 2015, he was derided for his statement and later apologized for it.[86]

An August 2015 poll showed that 78 percent of voters polled believed that the slogan "All Lives Matter" closely resembles their views on the subject, while 11 percent supported the "Black Lives Matter" phrase. Some have argued that using the phrase "All Lives Matter" is an attempt to silence Blacks who subscribe to what "Black Lives Matter" represents. Despite criticism of both slogans, their existence reflects the ability of Americans to speak their minds, show their dissent about social practices, and rally around a cause in which they believe. A comprehensive and inclusive campaign took hold as movement organizers partnered with other intersectional groups to broaden the movement's reach under the name of diversity and globalism. It employed a social media strategy as well as direct action in order to drive the advocates' points home.

### Toppling and Protesting of Monuments

In 2016 and 2017, protesters called for the removal of statues and other monuments that glorified the Confederacy. Statues of

Robert E. Lee, the commander of the Confederate States Army; of George Washington; and other prominent figures in history have been removed because the individuals they represent supported slavery centuries ago. Protest groups have exercised their rights to dissent from accepted policies of the past. Across America, statues of individuals and monuments to history have been removed because they represent a time when now-objectionable policies were enacted and accepted. From Baltimore, Maryland, to Seattle, Washington, monuments have been removed, though some would deem it political correctness gone mad.[87]

Perhaps encouraged by a white supremacist rally in Charlottesville, Virginia, that instigated a counter rally in 2017, Americans exercised their free speech and assembly rights to demand monument removal and dissent to policies that have kept the monuments in place.

US colleges and universities have also seen their fair share of protests related to race. In 2016, a group of Princeton University students objected to a portrait hung on campus of Woodrow Wilson, the university's thirteenth president (1902-1910), who later became the twenty-eighth president of the United States. Students staged a thirty-two-hour sit-in, also demanding that Princeton change the name of the Woodrow Wilson School of International Affairs.[88] A year earlier, protesters at Yale University demanded that the university change the name of a residential college named after John C. Calhoun, the seventh vice president of the United States and a staunch defender of slavery. Their protest succeeded.[89]

*National Football League Protests*

Though the 2017 protests by NFL players are mentioned throughout this book, they're worthy of a separate discussion. Started

*Saving Patriotism*

by former San Francisco 49er quarterback Colin Kaepernick, a man who, as a child, was given up for adoption by a white mother and adopted by a white family,[90] and who had an absentee father of African American descent,[91] the protest in support of better treatment of Blacks in America grew to affect all NFL teams. The NFL has a "rule" requiring players to stand at attention while the anthem is played or performed but declined to take any action against players who knelt or sat during the anthem. The protest took on larger proportions when President Trump weighed in, calling for the firing of any player demonstrating against the National Anthem or the American flag. Calling the demonstrations anti-American and making the protest about the anthem and flag, President Trump framed the issue in such a way that resulted in a drop-off of NFL game attendance, the destruction of football team jerseys and tickets, and public opinion turning against the players and teams, thus in support of the American anthem and flag.

Duane Locknane, a seventy-six-year-old former football player, three-year letterman at the University of Washington, and Seattle businessman, has commented extensively about the controversy, expressing a traditional view of patriotism. He played on the 1960 National Championship team and at the 1961 Rose Bowl under legendary coach Jim Owens. Duane graduated with degrees in industrial relations and marketing and joined the manufacturing company his dad had started back in 1946. After fifty years in the business, Duane and his wife, Susie, turned it over to their son, Brent, who started the business's thriving third generation.

Duane resides happily in Seattle and describes himself as a patriot who loves America but is concerned for its future — especially if coming generations have a negative view of patriotism and fail to love the United States as Duane and others do. He laments what America is experiencing — big changes that seem to ignore the past, with uncertainty about the future. Living in America's polarized political climate is difficult for Duane and many others who agree with his attitudes regarding patriotism, protest, and dissent, especially by athletes.

Duane's father served in World War II and his cousin, a Navy pilot, lost his life when his plane crashed while practicing aircraft carrier landings. Duane lost several friends in the Vietnam War, so he's had vicarious experiences that influence his point of view. As a younger man, he was infused with a traditional sense of patriotism by parents and others who influenced his life. Today he becomes emotional when he sees the Iwo Jima Memorial, watches the American flag being raised, observes the Changing of the Guard at the Tomb of the Unknown Soldier, and recites the Pledge of Allegiance.

As a father, he's tried to instill patriotic feelings in the younger generation and he's done so successfully. He laments that many younger people today care more for jobs that signal "success" and that monetary rewards are deemed so important. He says that people don't fully recognize the commitment to country of prior generations of Americans, whose sacrifice paved the way for a newer generation's financial success.

Duane Locknane is not alone, for many other Americans lament similar circumstances and worry for the perpetuation of American democracy as they've known it. A visit to the beaches of Normandy helps bring to the fore American sacrifice, a sacrifice Duane doesn't see as much of in today's polarized society. Many who love America in the tradition of the past share his feelings. Their views should be honored because they've stood the test of time — those views are born of wisdom and experience and, in many cases, the direct experience of sacrifice.

While Colin Kaepernick has every right to protest and call

attention to the treatment of Blacks in the US, particularly by police, Duane and many others believe he should honor the National Anthem and flag — in a traditional sense — and find another way to express his anger at racism. While Duane Locknane supports constitutionally protected free speech, he believes exercising that right should never disrespect the national symbols that allow it. In doing so, he's aligned himself with President Trump, who has made American athletic protests a national issue well discussed and analyzed from a variety of perspectives.

Dissent as patriotism is a longstanding American tradition; history is filled with moments where patriotic Americans, young and old, protested against government action and changed history. While it may not be the "purest" form of patriotism, as expressed by Jefferson, it is nevertheless an important and essential right of true democracy, freedom, and liberty, the kind that Americans for generations have fought to preserve.

CHAPTER 5

# DEFINING CIVICS AND ITS ELEMENTS

*"A constitutional democracy is in
serious trouble if its citizenry does not have
a certain degree of education and civic virtue."*
–Phillip E. Johnson

There are six major elements integral to the study of civics and civic learning that lead to patriotic feelings:

1. US history
2. Economics
3. Government
4. Foreign policy
5. Current affairs
6. Citizen involvement

Each is important to the study of civics, and each is relevant to the development of American citizens in regard to community engagement, long-term benefit, and civic literacy. They are all integrated with one another and are essential elements of a robust American citizenship that results in greater patriotism and a healthier democracy.

## US History

In order for American citizens to appreciate the essence of the American system, it is essential that they understand the country's history. Jamaican publisher and activist Marcus Garvey once said, "A people without the knowledge of past history, origin, and culture is like a tree without roots." The history of the United States rivals the drama of any novel; it's filled with stories of triumph and tragedy, sacrifice and salvation, struggles and successes. It is the story of overcoming internal and external challenges, of righting wrongs, of conferring rights — and protecting them — and of maximizing freedom and minimizing oppression.

The beauty of American history is discovering what America has been through as a nation, learning from it, daring not as a country to repeat its actionable setbacks and mistakes, and always progressing within the parameters of America's most dynamic and important founding document — the Constitution. Famous author and historian David McCullough, a civic-learning advocate, has likened students of today to "cut flowers — beautiful and colorful, but without roots." Roots and history comprise the elements of civic learning and patriotism. They're essential to fully understanding America and being a contributing citizen.

When US presidents and public officials are sworn in to the offices to which they've been freely elected or appointed, they pledge no allegiance to their government — they pledge allegiance to the Constitution, the longest-surviving constitution of any in history. Knowing how it was developed, how numerous judges have interpreted it, and its application to every American's daily life is priceless. Founding father Thomas Jefferson once said, "It would be a dangerous delusion were a confidence in the men of our choice to silence our fears for the safety of our rights . . ." By this quote,

Jefferson underscored his belief that ours is a government of laws, not men, a founding principle that has served the American people well since its adoption.

That's why electing people of accomplishment and high moral principles is so significant for America's future. The founding principles contained in the Bill of Rights (e.g., the importance of the right to vote); the Gettysburg ideal that "government of the people, by the people and for the people shall not perish from the earth"; and the principles underscored by the Constitution's Twenty-seventh Amendment are what has kept the United States growing, maturing, and cultivating a more just society. If these concepts are not known and understood by US citizens, America cannot continue to exist as it has for 243 years. US history is a series of dramatic stories told from various perspectives that rightly give Americans the understanding of who they are. These stories help us understand our country's public policies, many of which were enacted after long, arduous battles. US history, the Constitution, freedom, and civics are nearly synonymous.

*Economics*

The US economic system is based on the idea that free markets and capitalism are the best ways for Americans to apply their respective talents and allow their innovation to meet public demand, thus creating jobs and opportunities for others. The American economic story has always been about innovation, creating and producing ideas and products to better mankind, and helping Americans pursue inventions, as evidenced by intellectual property and patents being protected under the Constitution.

From inventing the electric light bulb and the electronic computer to manufacturing the automobile and transcontinental airplanes, not to mention developing ground travel and space travel, Americans have been at the forefront of technology and innovation, using the capitalist model to unleash the ingenuity of the human mind and lead the world. The American economy has created astonishing medical technologies that extend lifespans and limit human suffering; it has created an economy per capita that dwarfs the economies of many other nations and governmental systems. Americans must understand free-market capitalism, the proper role of government in spurring economies, the financial consequences of taxation and the national debt, the relationship of international trade to economic growth, and the consequences of too much — or too little — government regulation if we are going to elect leaders who will safeguard national prosperity.

Microsoft founder Bill Gates once said, "Capitalism has worked very well. Anyone who wants to move to North Korea is welcome." Understanding capitalism, its abuses and successes, and its history is necessary for any American who wants to be civically knowledgeable and informed. The dangers of not being knowledgeable about how our economy works have been evident in the increasing gap between the wealthiest Americans and the vanishing middle class.

## *Government*

Understanding government for the average American is an onerous task. There's almost no book one can read to fully inform the reader about how the massive federal government works. With thirteen hundred agencies, more than two million employees, and a staggering budget of some four trillion dollars, the federal government has grown far beyond the founding fathers' wildest imaginations. One member of the 114th Session of Congress (the House) now represents about 768,000 people, the population of each congressional district. In the first Congress, convened from 1789 to 1791, there were sixty-five House members, each representing sixty thousand people per district, when the total population of the country was 3.9 million. The population in 2018 was about 325 million, and there were 435 members in the House.

The US Department of Defense is headquartered at the Pentagon, a five-sided building that houses some twenty-three thousand employees dedicated to keeping the United States and its citizens safe from attack. It is the headquarters for all military planning and deployment decisions around the world. It implements an annual federal budget of nearly one trillion dollars and is responsible for a procurement budget of nearly one hundred fifty billion annually. Procurement for defense includes the acquisition of fighter jets, warships, trucks, missiles, and other equipment, including thousands of component parts to keep America's military modernized so it can remain the best in the world and can protect Americans and our allies across the globe. While some Americans have disputed the need for a modern defense budget that approaches one trillion dollars, defense of the United States has been an essential government function since America's War for Independence and, later, the War of 1812, the first serious attack from another nation on America's newly formed government.

Government functions to ensure a steady and safe food supply for citizens (US Department of Agriculture), the collection of taxes to fund the government (IRS), the minting of money for commercial transactions, the construction and maintenance of a transnational highway system to allow citizens to traverse the fifty states (Department of Transportation), and the creation of a national legislature and maintenance of a federal court system to adopt and interpret the laws of the land. Our government is massive because the United States is immense and its people have massive national needs.

Government is an essential function of a free society; it binds the country and the nearly 330 million people who reside here. As previously mentioned, "e pluribus unum," America's national motto, stands for "out of many, one." Out of many people, one national legislature, one president, and one Supreme Court determine the affairs of Americans through one federal government. Because government is so prominent in American lives, it is essential that citizens understand its basic civic details.

## Foreign Policy

The United States has rarely been an island unto itself, free from entanglements with other nations, notwithstanding its unique positioning on the North American continent with rich natural resources and two vast oceans protecting its borders. Its foreign policy was developed over the course of two world wars, forty-five presidents, more than ten thousand members of Congress, economic downturns and upswings, and relationships fostered and broken among the world's 195 nations.[92]

Foreign policy knowledge is tricky — the policy oftentimes changes as American leaders change. In 2012, American foreign policy occasionally came under attack. One example was massive demonstrations in the oil-rich Middle East after the release of a film considered highly insulting to Islamic beliefs. The American ambassador to Libya and three staffers there were killed amid the protests. But American foreign policy has traditionally supported freedom — not just for Americans, but also for others seeking it.

The wars in Iraq and Afghanistan that began in 2003 are recent examples. The US has also served as an ultimate bulwark against oppression, intervening in countries where the people were fighting for freedom from oppressive governments. That policy has sometimes led to war, conflict, and turmoil, but it has been largely unyielding as an American foreign policy — that of helping the people of other nations achieve freedom.

The North American Treaty Organization (NATO), created in 1949, has since WWII been a means of uniting countries that value individual freedom in support of each other in their quest to be free from attack and in support of international quests for freedom. Other American pronouncements since 1776, such as the Monroe Doctrine in 1823, have served as notices to other nations of American limits on foreign aggression and set standards opposing action against the United States and its interests and allies. If citizens and leaders are ignorant of such a history of foreign affairs, they cannot be fully engaged in understanding modern relationships between nations.

The world is shrinking, and America has, in recent decades, become far more multicultural. Ethnic diversity is now evident in urban and rural areas of America. A recent study found 46.3 million Americans aged fourteen to twenty-four to be the most diverse generation in America today.[93] Other sources peg the number of languages spoken in the US in 2012 at 311. As America has become more diverse, and if citizens are to be civically literate, they need to know about American foreign policy and the relations other countries have with the US. As the US population changes to include many cultures, without continued emphasis on the lessons of history and the values fought for, new populations and new cultures will be uninformed about the common values that have shaped America.

Leaders setting American foreign policy who lack a sense of American history will be unprepared to perpetuate a policy that has served the country well for many generations.

That's why congressional leaders steeped in a broad knowledge of foreign relations history and historical interactions of the world's major nations are so important for just and effective foreign policy.

Foreign policy formed with a knowledge of world history is essential to a patriotic nation. In a global age, knowledge of countries and cultures throughout the world is essential.

## *Current Affairs*

Current affairs become yesterday's news and eventually history as communications continue to modernize and proliferate. Television now boasts more than five hundred channels,[94] all outlets seeking to capture audience share with a different twist on programming. But even with an abundance of twenty-four-hour news stations and news outlets across the internet, the task of being fully informed about current affairs has been challenging for the average citizen, and there is ample evidence that too many Americans are ignorant of current events.

Yet, good citizenship requires a basic level of knowledge of political, social, cultural, business, economic, foreign, governmental, entertainment, sports, and world affairs. Elected officials and candidates for public office must be particularly knowledgeable on many topics of the day, enough that their knowledge can be reassuring to the citizens they represent or seek to represent in government.

Because of the wide array of broadcast options, the temptation for many is to watch mindless shows — sitcoms, game shows, cooking programs, talent and reality shows, and sports. It's no wonder that, of the most-watched prime-time television programs in 2018, only one was about current events (*60 Minutes*). The rest were escapist viewing for the mindless viewer who is too lazy, too busy, or too disinterested to watch current events on television. It's lamentable that more Americans can name the *American Idol* judges than can name the Supreme Court Justices![95] It may be that

Americans' lives are so busy for so many reasons that too many don't want to focus on politics or current affairs — they're another source of worry and distress.

Studying civics could change that, however. More Americans are urging a greater emphasis on civic learning. Harvard University's *Harvard Magazine* published a 2012 article entitled "Renewing civic education — Time to restore American higher education's lost mission."[96] Written by former Harvard deans Ellen Condliffe Lagemann and Harry R. Lewis, the article speaks of the importance of citizens gaining wisdom and knowledge by the study of the effect of human decisions on the welfare of others. In the fast-paced world of current events, decisions are made that affect human conditions, and further actions affect those decisions already made. It is in the interest of all Americans to make current affairs an essential part of their daily lives.

*Citizen Involvement*

The final component of the elements of civics requires even more activism. The aforementioned article in *Harvard Magazine* calls on academia broadly to take responsibility for restoring higher education's lost mission: civic education of all students, regardless of their chosen field of study or academic specialty. The authors argue that "the need for civic education is urgent because so many aspects of our civic life have become dysfunctional." Further, they assert that America's republican form of government will not persist "through momentum alone" and that civic education cultivates knowledge and traits that "sustain democratic self-governance." As veterans of academia, Lagemann and Lewis not only identify the problem of too little civic literacy, but they offer an academic solution, naming their view of the components of civic education in colleges and universities as a "tripod of intellect, morality, and action, all grounded in a knowledge base of American history and constitutional principles."

In short, history and the Constitution are not just social studies topics; they're teachable from any discipline. A science professor can incorporate analysis of the morality of scientific discovery with the social consequences thereof; a computer programming course can examine the relative greater good of technological development for society.

Instilling students with a sense of the common good can and should be included in any course of study. The fact that academic specialization since the 1960s has choked out civic learning in teaching has failed the higher-education purpose, but it has also shortchanged student learning, as more students find themselves civically illiterate and society finds itself lacking a moral foundation and understanding of the meaning of the common good. This has played a significant role in the polarization of the country, and it is eroding our democracy, pitting American against American as we fail to even try to find common ground and compromise.

Lagemann and Lewis offer a framework for a national academic conversation about the roles intellect, morality, and action play in student development and the potential of universities to (1) integrate civic education into core requirements and concentrations of study (students' majors), (2) encourage students to think not only of getting a job after graduation, but also contributing to the world's future by joining organizations such as the Peace Corps and AmeriCorps, and (3) serve as role models for civic engagement, embodying solid values in all operations of university administration. The authors argue for these measures, suggesting that the consequences of academia's failure to reinvigorate civic learning are carrying and will continue to carry a "high price" that risks the well-being of the

United States.

Service learning is a way for students to incorporate inside of class what they learn outside. It is an effective way to engage students in the "real-life" experiences of America and offers a platform for students to put into practice the theoretical principles of the American system of government. At Harvard and other prominent universities, students have the opportunity to teach grade school students about the Constitution and its important elements. Some Harvard students help tutor university employees who are seeking American citizenship. Some schools develop community projects to help solve a local problem, embrace a charitable organization, encourage volunteerism by creating a new idea to benefit a city or town, and devise ways to voluntarily help others in need.

American education can be a more prominent leader in cultivating good citizens if we see the value of developing the "whole" student — not just the academic qualities, but the moral ones as well. Lawyers can visit more classrooms to explain the American justice system; grandparents, by their active example, can encourage their grandchildren to get into the habit of helping others; and individuals of all occupations can relate their work to a cultural or moral lesson for the younger generation.

Citizen activism can be a catalyst for civic learning. If the "material haves" of a community offer themselves to the "material have-nots" to make a community better (e.g., clean up a public street, erase graffiti, remove litter from a local park, repaint a community center, etc.), think what a message doing so would send to younger generations about self-help and caring for others. Think what eyes would be opened to those with and without material possessions. Think how true civic engagement would foster other civic engagements to better society and bridge gaps between Americans.

Wisdom, knowledge virtue, and selfless action are qualities most humans admire — and want to replicate — for the common good. According to TechNet, replication behavior is predictable and consistent. We must also convince millennials and Gen Zers who have finished their educations of the importance of civic engagement. A younger citizen, armed with knowledge and a commitment to a cause, can change the world through activism. If people don't like the state of public affairs, they should become active against that to which they object, educating themselves to similar causes and becoming armed with historical facts and strategies to understand how to achieve their aims — on gun control and climate change, for instance, to choose two topical issues. It was heartening to see high school and college students march across the country in 2018 to protest the lack of gun control, as well as to see scientists march to protest the country's rolling back of measures intended to temper climate change.

"Defining Civics" was the topic at the all-day conference in 2017 in DC sponsored by iCivics, the Hewlett Foundation, the Robert R. McCormick Foundation, and the Carnegie Corporation of New York, among others. The conference title was "Democracy at a Crossroads." Its mission was to bring together for discussion civic learning experts from across America at a national summit to discuss the state of American democracy and propose ways to bolster it through a greater emphasis on civic learning.

Sessions included State of Our Democracy: What's at Stake; Policy Innovation: Getting Results from Renewing a Commitment to Civic Education; How Civic Learning Got Its Groove Back: Demand, Proof, and Innovation in Today's Classrooms; Civic Learning Across the Divide; Teaching the Rules of the Game: Why Invest in Civic Education; Next Generation Democracy; Making the Case for Civic Education: Why We Must Act Now; Digital Engagement: Gaming; News and Young People; Laying the Groundwork for Equity in Our

Democracy; and Civic Commitments to Action. National Civic Learning Awards for Exceptional Service were made, and US Supreme Court Justice Sonia Sotomayor was interviewed and took audience questions. A Supreme Court reception followed.

The overwhelming conclusion is that the American republic is at risk, and civics is part of the solution. The Annenberg Public Policy Center, a summit sponsor, in August 2017 conducted a national survey of 1,013 American adults, finding that 53 percent thought that people in the country illegally don't have any constitutional rights; 37 percent couldn't name any of the rights guaranteed by the First Amendment to the Constitution; and only 26 percent could name all three branches of government, down from 35 percent only a few years ago.

The iCivics organization and several others[97] found deep distrust of the federal government and declining trust in organized religion, public schools, banks, organized labor, big business, and the media, finding further that Americans mistrust their fellow citizens, believing that the republic is ungovernable. One in three have at least a good deal of confidence in the wisdom of the American people in political decision-making, down substantially over the past twenty years.

Additional findings included deep distrust of those who weren't aligned with their political party, signaling a deep philosophical division among Americans. That polarization extends to political institutions and particularly to young adults (millennials), 35 percent of whom have declared that they're losing faith in American democracy, with only 25 percent who were confident in the democratic system. Harvard University's survey recently found that 25 percent of its students were not planning to vote; they, like too many other Americans, have lost faith in the system and don't believe they have the power to do anything about it.

Without question, these and other statistics reflect the toxic environment in which public policy is made. Those at the conference concluded that many Americans don't possess the levels of skill, literacy, and training essential to participate in American life and that civic learning is an essential part of the solution. When done properly, civic learning can be the best vehicle for training young people — the next generation — to sustain our democracy and perpetuate the principles that Americans hold dear. Bringing people together so that the rich understand the poor better, the white population better understands minorities in America, and men understand women, can benefit all and lead to more understanding — of power, critical thinking, and collaboration — that advances knowledge and civic advocacy.

The conference endorsed openmindedness, calling for greater tolerance among Americans of differing points of view. It also surfaced the lack of basic skills of too many students: how to write an email and understand what a graph is, for example. Further, it found a difference of opinion as to the value of testing: some approved of tests but called for updating them each year; others believed that facts taught merely to pass a test are rarely retained and that development of critical thinking is longer lasting. It was acknowledged that many Americans get their news online and that fake news, which has been detected on numerous websites, is equal to deliberate lying and is thus unacceptable; that a political climate change is necessary; and schools may be the best place for civic learning because students are a captive audience.

Yet, some states and schools are unenlightened about civic learning, instead adopting STEM subjects as a priority, or a preferred curriculum. It was believed that a coalition of civic learning supporters is necessary to influence policy makers, including educators, to support civic learning as a national priority. However, there must be a common background so that young people are exposed to power and understand how it works. Many young people won't receive civic learning today as their parents are undereducated or disinterested. It is difficult to infuse young Americans with an understanding of power and empathy in a way that gives them an attachment to their country — their private interests will equal their public interests as they become civically literate, having developed civic skills and knowledge.

It's important to understand that the US immigration test, whereby applicants must study one hundred questions, are quizzed on ten of them, and must answer six out of ten correctly, is not a very rigorous civics test. Nor does it define what all Americans must know to be civically literate. The USCIS examiner conducts the quiz orally so that the examiner can determine whether an applicant can read, write, and understand English.

Civic learning involves judgment combined with knowledge, empathy, and an understanding of power. Some immigrant applicants for citizenship feel at risk because they don't have a strong command of the English language or understand the concepts of power or empathy in the American system. It's the job of tutors or others charged with educating and preparing immigrant applicants for citizenship to help them understand such concepts. Communicating well will help immigrant applicants become good citizens, and helping them understand how American society works will help them better define civics. Indeed, education gives us knowledge of the world, increases our earning ability, and helps us become an "interesting person." It will also help overcome the cynicism of the 25 percent of Americans who have lost faith in government institutions.

There are numerous organizations to assist in civic learning for all, helping recipients understand the concepts of power and empathy.

Some include the American Bar Association, the Annenberg Public Policy Corporation, the Federal Bar Association, the League of Women Voters, the Reagan Institute, and others, many of which sponsored the "Democracy at a Crossroads" civics conference.

Civics education must include US history, economics, government, and foreign policy but can also include knowing how to be a better American citizen. Generation Citizen, a nonprofit organization focused on an action civics curriculum, has made numerous findings about the sorry state of civic learning in America, yet strives to define, teach, and emphasize the importance of civics so that every American student receives the knowledge and skills necessary to be an active, participatory citizen in American democracy — and so that young people gain confidence and understand that they can make a difference locally, nationally, and even globally.

The Boy Scouts of America (BSA) awards a Citizenship in the Nation Merit Badge (all Eagle Scouts must earn it) to all scouts who meet the badge's requirements, including learning about America and how to become a good citizen. A new patch (the American Civics Knowledge Award) for possessing advanced knowledge of America is being offered to scouts and scout troops at no cost.

The US Citizenship and Immigration Services (USCIS), the federal agency that controls immigrant citizenship applications, is interested in developing a tutoring program for applicants to help prepare them for American citizenship. The Association of Former Members of Congress has made civic learning an important part of its efforts to engage former members to help others learn about civics. School districts are encouraged to adopt a senior-to-senior program whereby seniors in high school interview senior citizens so each can learn from the other and foster connections between generations of Americans.

While there are other valuable programs not mentioned here that strive to connect Americans with their history and an understanding of how US history, economics, government, and foreign policy work in the United States, defining civics continues to be a work in progress that will determine America's future course to enhance patriotism and preserve a vibrant democracy.

There are entities that help Americans understand their government from an early age. Other entities perform similar services designed to connect Americans with their heritage in an effort to help Americans learn about freedom, the Constitution (which guides American policy), and the precious nature of liberty that is the cornerstone and basis for the government Americans have enjoyed since the United States was formed. Despite all the great work being done by a host of organizations and individuals, there remains a lack of national consensus — and action — on the imperative of restoring civic education to our schools and universities. We need teachers' unions, school boards, school superintendents, state boards of education, and university administrators to buy into the need for civic education and get it back in our classrooms.

CHAPTER 6

# FROM CIVICS TO PATRIOTISM

*"Take patriotism away and the nation's soul has fled."*
–Edward Mark Deems

Civic learning can result in patriotic feelings in Americans and therefore lead to patriotism, but how do we get there? When an American studies the history of our country's independence and the sacrifices of others for future generations, they cannot help but be impressed that others had foresight, hope, and determination about the American experiment.

Patriotism has been at the core of the success of this country at home and abroad, in peace and in war. The American way has been largely successful, even though in retrospect we wonder how prior generations could have tolerated the treatment of some segments of society — Black Americans, who were enslaved and, after emancipation, suffered terrible discrimination and violence; women, who weren't granted the right to vote until 1920; whites and Blacks who married and faced the prospect of incarceration; gays who also could not marry and also faced discrimination — to name a few.

This country has made terrible mistakes at home and abroad.

But we're working on righting longstanding wrongs. In each instance, it was the citizens of the country standing up to government that finally got our leaders to change policies and the people to change attitudes. These successful protestors were patriots, and they understood how government works and how to effect significant policy changes. They were civically literate.

The Fund for American Studies (TFAS) is one of many groups in America that instills a sense of patriotism in young people that can last a lifetime. It celebrated its fiftieth year in 2017 and has a track record of accomplishment, counting prominent alumni such as former editor-in-chief of the *Weekly Standard*, Steve Hayes, and ABC news anchor David Muir among some sixteen thousand people worldwide who have gone through the program.[98] In 2017, Supreme Court Justice Neal Gorsuch addressed TFAS about the dual importance of teaching civics and encouraging habits of civility (see chapter 2). It is through organizations such as TFAS that others hear the civic learning message that leads to patriotism. Each year, TFAS gives an award to a prominent individual who exemplifies the spirit of patriotism that TFAS encourages.

In September 2017, Garry Kasparov, Russian-Croatian chess champion and Soviet defector to America, received the Walter Judd Freedom Award from TFAS.[99] In his acceptance speech, Kasparov gave a ringing endorsement of freedom and America's role in perpetuating it. His speech was moving.

To pause and recognize the nature of American democracy, however, is to acknowledge that the legislative process is extremely cumbersome — by design. It frustrates many Americans because it's so slow. Congress often seems paralyzed by the process. But, once it's understood, the pathway to patriotism is easier.

Once a bill is introduced, it passes to a committee of jurisdiction for consideration. Either the House of Representatives or the Senate, or both, considers it, sometimes reporting it out with a committee's or subcommittee's changes or other considerations. If there are both House and Senate versions, members of the Committee of Jurisdiction meet to hammer out any differences in a Conference

Committee, reporting a final version to each body for consideration without amendment.

Once that version of the conference committee report is voted upon with possible amendments, if it passes, it's sent to the president of the United States for either signature or veto. If vetoed by the president while Congress is in session, each body can overcome the veto by a two-thirds vote, and if the veto is overridden, the measure becomes law. If the president does nothing after ten days with Congress in session, a measure becomes law. If a veto is forthcoming, usually the president will signal a veto to Congress.

So, the pathway from civics to patriotism can be cumbersome. Implementation of laws is not usually easy or swift. That can be frustrating to American presidents, legislators, and citizens alike. Oftentimes we want policies changed quickly, but the American system calls for deliberation and patience, and the founding fathers designed it that way so that passions of the moment would not overtake sound judgment and wisdom. Presidents can and do encourage passage of legislation, though they cannot introduce legislative measures: only Congress can.

The House of Representatives is subject to new elections every two years because it is closest to the people, allowing voters to frequently change representatives if they desire. On the other hand, the Senate, terms of which last six years, is deemed a place for passions to cool and sober deliberations to take hold. The Senate acts as the final arbiter of the people's passions, expressed through their representatives. The president is the third barrier. However, recognizing that the American government is one of process, the people (represented by their elected officials) are able to override the president's judgment about legislation. When a presidential veto is overridden, the people (again, through their representatives) remain in charge. One person alone, even the president, cannot decide what's good for the entire country. The government consists of checks and balances to all who make official decisions so that one branch of government can never be fully dominant — each branch is able to check the others.

Understanding the legislative process leads you from citizenship to patriotism as you recognize the genius of the legislative system, embrace it, and then participate in public policy matters. But the genius of the system can only be recognized if it's understood. That's why reading the founding documents is so important.

The president plays an important role in this process. That role is to act as another voice for the people, in addition to the legislative branch and its role as "legislature-in-chief." The president's formal role is to implement national laws through the government agencies that have jurisdiction over an issue. The president can also issue executive orders, and recent presidents have exercised that right in order to circumvent Congress.

It is assumed that federal legislators are good citizens and patriots, too. Most are. As representatives of millions of citizens, they are expected to know more about US history, government, economics, and foreign policy than the ordinary citizen since they have massive information available to them instantly and they work in government each day, unlike the citizens they represent.

The Senate has twenty committees, sixty-eight subcommittees, and four joint committees. The House has twenty-five committees, one hundred four subcommittees, and four joint committees. Oftentimes the staff members Congress hires earn their passage from citizenship to patriotism through exposure to governmental issues — they gain an understanding of how government works. Their education is unique and not available to every citizen. That's why they must keep in mind that the citizen has immense power: the power of the vote. The public often assumes that lobbyists wield the most power in the nation's capital, but their power pales in comparison to that held by the voter. Too often, either staff members or their bosses — the members of Congress — forget that voters decide whether an elected representative is able to continue to serve.

If staff or congressional members take themselves too seriously, in the process forgetting the fundamental relationship of who works for whom, constituents become upset. That is the case particularly when their representatives act against their and the majority's interests and lose faith in the American system of government. It's a block in the pathway to citizenship and patriotism.

Since the 2012 massacre at Sandy Hook, for instance, a majority of Americans have supported stricter gun control laws, and a 2018 *Washington Post*-ABC News poll found that 62 percent of Americans favored banning assault weapons. And yet most state legislatures and Congress have done nothing to control the proliferation of guns.

Elected officials have been recently reluctant to afford constituents access to them for "town hall" meetings for fear of disruption by a public angry over lack of legislative progress. Distrust and unprecedented hostility of one party toward the other have impeded the passage of important legislation, and often it seems one party stymies the legislation proposed by the other side out of spite, not policy differences.

The first female Supreme Court Justice, Sandra Day O'Connor, once suggested that congressional votes be held late Friday and early Monday so that members would stay in Washington, DC, over a weekend and "get to know each other," thereby perhaps fostering compromise and making the way from citizenship to patriotism easier.

But Congress has changed. No longer do Democrats and Republicans fraternize as they once did. The fault lies in the polarization that exists in government today. That's because the pathway to patriotism comes from sincere and effective communication, respect for the ideas of others, and compromise without sacrificing one's principles. Compromise has come to be defined as "lacking in principles." But compromise was what the founding fathers did when America was formed; it's how the Vietnam War was ended. Compromise is how legislative disagreements are resolved. Some of the most significant policy changes in America occurred only because both parties were willing to compromise to get the job done.

Sometimes principles take a back seat to politics. When the Affordable Care Act (ACA, or Obamacare) came before the House of Representatives for a vote, no Republicans supported it, so it passed and became law with only Democratic votes (never appropriate for major legislation). Likewise, Republican changes to the ACA under President Trump received no Democratic support. When the ACA passed the House, a Michigan Democrat and fine member of Congress voted in favor, in spite of the ACA's violating his pro-life principles. The member soon resigned from the House, a tragic loss to good government.

But it doesn't only happen in Democratic administrations. When President Bush held office, pressure to support anti-textile legislation was imposed on a North Carolina Republican House member who wanted to oppose it but couldn't vote against the president of his own party. He was defeated in the next election.

Too often in today's legislative world, politics gets in the way of principle. In 2017, forty-five Senate Democrats voted against confirmation of Justice Neal Gorsuch, by most nonpartisan accounts a highly qualified nominee. Their reason was largely partisan because of their strong dislike for President Trump. He was confirmed anyway. But there are countless examples of one party or the other standing in the way of potentially beneficial legislation to spite the other party. And when they do, they further erode the trust of the people, and cynicism sets in all around.

Patriotism is at work when policy makers compromise, recognizing that there is more than one way or policy that's correct for America, with its diverse populace.

The pathway from civics to patriotism requires an element of statesmanship, of doing what is right for America regardless of the political benefits or consequences. When now-deceased Alaska senator Ted Stevens was in office (1968-2009), he had a campaign slogan: "To hell with politics — just do what's right."[100] It served him well, as he became the longest-serving Republican in history — forty years — and rose to become a Senate leader and chair of the Senate Appropriations Committee.

And as Senator Cory Booker, a Democrat from New Jersey, put it in a speech to the Democratic National Convention in 2016, "Patriotism is love of country. But you can't love your country without loving your countrymen and women. We don't always have to agree, but we must empower each other; we must find the common ground; we must build bridges across our differences to pursue the common good."[101]

CHAPTER 7

# How Citizenship and Patriotism Grow

*"To be a good patriot, a man must consider his countrymen as God's creatures and himself as accountable for his acting towards them."*
–Bishop Berkeley

Citizenship and patriotism should be like the love of a spouse or a parent — enduring, never in doubt, constant. Though divorces occur and families become disrupted, the feeling of never-ending commitment should be the feeling we have for our country.

American patriotism should not be questioned. We Americans have a civic obligation to be patriots; we should be thankful that we're able to reside in a freedom-loving nation, one that looks out for the individual and often the less fortunate in American society.

Welfare spending as a matter of national commitment has soared since first enacted, now exceeding one trillion dollars per year.[102] That's because policy makers have cared for those of limited means, subsidizing housing, food, and general welfare, believing that it is government's responsibility to look out for those least able to support themselves. Food stamps were devised to help the hungry. The homeless can receive government help, but also charitable assistance, provided by Americans voluntarily, because they care for those with less in our society. The National Alliance to End Homelessness reported that government spending to combat homelessness in 2015 was $4.5 billion. The United States has a strong and lengthy legacy of helping those in need, at home and abroad.

When Cuba, which America imposed a largely unilateral embargo against in 1959, suffered hurricane destruction early in the twenty-first century, the United States was there to offer food and other material assistance. When Haiti suffered a devastating earthquake in 2010, among those who stepped up to lead the recovery effort there, raising millions, were two former US presidents, one having defeated the other in the 1992 national election. Such is the nature of the country some 330 million people call home — America of the twenty-first century.

Helping others cultivates good citizenship and patriotism. When we help others, we help ourselves. It is something that should be ingrained in all Americans, regardless of the natural ups and downs of American politics. We can easily be upset with and protest the actions of our government (dissenting is patriotic — see chapter 4) but we should support our country, always striving to make it better, and to help others. Under the American system, Americans elect our "best and brightest" as the people's representatives — as members of the House and Senate — and expect them to make good decisions on all Americans' behalf.

One of the vital obligations we citizens have is that of choosing our representatives wisely, voting at election time, and learning about how government operates so we can knowledgeably criticize, support, or otherwise provide feedback on the decisions of our leaders. After all, it's the citizens' country, and the president and Congress are America's employees, entrusted to represent the collective interests of all.

Sadly, politicians too often fail to represent their constituents well, instead worrying about their own welfare (raising reelection money) and financial security and hanging onto their public positions. Politicians don't share the economic uncertainties facing the public — they're assured of a paycheck and health insurance as long as they hold office. More officeholders should be subject to the same economic ups and downs as the society they represent. Then perhaps more of them would act in the best interests of all Americans, not just those who contribute to their campaigns.

Though at times it is appropriate to criticize officeholders, many exhibit a patriotic attitude from which we can learn. Many express patriotic words and conduct patriotic acts worthy of any good citizen. The best kind of citizen patriot in public office is one who feels the draw of history, strives to pass on patriotic lessons to those he or she represents, and acts in a statesmanlike manner. It's a person who conducts himself or herself with the dignity due the office and shows the public that he or she cares about the well-being of our nation.

One way to nurture citizenship and patriotism is for elected officials to endorse patriotic actions, publicly recognize them in others, and make an example of good citizenship. Another is to pass laws requiring young people to master civic study, or advocate for college and university credits for civic study and actions. As of 2018, at least eight states required high school seniors to pass the US naturalization test in order to graduate from high school.

Other states also require some form of civic learning. A third way is to have student tutors assist applicants for naturalization so that the tutors learn as much about America as the immigrants they help. A fourth way is to establish gaming competition for civic learning via smartphones and other computer devices, allowing challenges to be issued, person to person, school to school, community to community. Citizenship and patriotism can then grow through exposure.

Growing patriotism and citizenship can assuredly be accomplished by activism, with federal, state, and local governments insisting on civics curriculum enhancement. Ideas about enhancing citizenship and patriotism start with our schools and can be the product of greater emphasis on civic learning. As mentioned, a number of Harvard University students tutor immigrant applicants for citizenship. At Harvard during a student visit for potential freshmen, a young woman from California who was considering attending either Stanford or Harvard mentioned that she had tutored her Jamaican parents for citizenship. She chose Harvard in part because of their tutoring program.

Civic learning has taken a back seat to STEM learning for a generation in our schools. While STEM subjects are critical to our future, civic learning is important, too. Fluency in math and science is necessary to a progressive society, but understanding the social and political consequences or benefits of such knowledge is essential for a society to make informed and compassionate decisions.

Some have suggested that voting is such an important citizenship element that it should be tied to one's civic knowledge — that if someone cannot pass the naturalization test, as we expect immigrant applicants to do in order to eventually cast a ballot, that person should not be able to vote. Though such a requirement would likely be challenged as unconstitutional, it nevertheless raises a provocative issue. If passage of the civics test is required of immigrant applicants so that they're knowledgeable of US history, government, and economic policies and can vote, what about the rest of us? Shouldn't America want educated voters? Too many citizens now cast ballots based on political party affiliation. With growing numbers of unaffiliated or independent voters, knowledge of issues and candidates is even more important. Requiring passage of a civics test to vote is unlikely to fly politically, but it remains worthy of consideration.

For years, the Nethercutt Foundation provided businesses in Spokane with free basic civics questions and answers to be used at weekly company staff meetings. The practice yielded more-informed citizens, inspired employees to consider the possibility of running for public office, and took only minutes. It's an easy way to educate citizens, encourage public service, and spread the word of the importance of civic learning. Years ago, the US Endowment for the Humanities conducted a study of the impact of civic learning on family health. The findings were that families that are civically learned are stronger. They vote more often, volunteer in their communities regularly, and are in turn better citizens.

Growing patriotism and citizenship is every citizen's responsibility. Bar associations, whose members are in the business of challenging, implementing, and making laws, should encourage lawyers to educate their clients about how laws are made, thereby helping citizens better understand America's governmental system.

After the Japanese attacked Pearl Harbor, which led to American entrance into World War II, America became united against an oppressive enemy. Personal sacrifice was standard. People from all walks and ages of life participated in the war effort. Efforts to nationally mobilize for war ensued. Blackouts in American cities were adhered to because Americans were united.[103] Military enrollments soared because Americans wanted to defend their nation. Women poured into factories to propel the war machine. Congress eagerly accepted President Roosevelt's call for a declaration of war. All Americans wanted to support their country. Patriotic songs proliferated on the radio, and American flags flew across the country.

While crisis and tragedy are not the most desirable ways to enhance patriotism and citizenship, Americans are quick to support their country and its leaders when common enemies strike against

*Saving Patriotism*

their nation. Likewise, when natural disasters strike America, citizens spring into action, helping those touched by disaster. Hurricane Harvey, which devastated Houston, Texas, and the people there, touched off a national giving effort totaling millions of dollars in excess of President Trump's declaration of disaster there, where federal dollars were provided for relief.

Patriotism is a natural byproduct of tragedy. It's like the old saying, "I can criticize my own family, but if you criticize them, I'll come to their aid and defend them." We can criticize our own nation, but if outsiders do, Americans will usually defend their country. That's patriotism. Outside criticism of America brings out the patriot in most Americans.

In 2017 and 2018 North Korea challenged America and the world with the threat of nuclear weapons.[104] A nuclear strike by North Korea, or by the United States against North Korea, would, of course, lead to a tragedy of epic proportions. All humans would be affected; people of all ages and stages in life, of all nationalities. While many Americans have rejected President Trump's approach to relations with North Korea, Americans supported their president and the officials around him both in standing up to North Korea and, later, agreeing to negotiate. At no time more so than in war or in the midst of a national tragedy do Americans understand the meaning of patriotism and the love of country. Those sentiments should translate into a renewed emphasis on civic knowledge in our schools.

The more we know of past sacrifices of Americans, the greater our citizenship and patriotism. Knowing our history makes us appreciate America and what she stands for; moreover, we learn just how precious the American system is. Presidents often speak about "our great country." There is a method to these utterances. President Ronald Reagan once said that his policies had to be repeated over and over to stick. Repeatedly emphasizing the greatness of America may turn skeptics into believers, thus enhancing patriotism and citizenship.

Educating our youth is the best way to ingrain in them patriotism and good citizenship. For instance, helping young people understand the difference between illegal and legal immigration and the rights and responsibilities of each is important. Many Americans object to undocumented immigration. Undocumented immigrants come to America not always to be Americans, but to be foreigners working and living in America. The goal is to get the younger set to support naturalization, not entry to America by undocumented means.

Speaking of President Reagan, he was known as the "Great Communicator."[105] He made statements that resonated with Americans and persuaded them to his point of view. His 1984 reelection effort proved it — he won forty-nine states and achieved a landslide victory. American psychologist Rollo May has been quoted as saying, "Communication leads to community — that is, to understanding, intimacy, and the mutual valuing that was previously lacking." Reagan's repeated emphasis on the greatness of America fostered that sense of community.

Communication is one of the great keys to the growth of citizenship and patriotism. Learning about their country helps people become better citizens as it arms them with a basic understanding of how the American system works. Reading the Constitution and Declaration of Independence is a good starting point, for these founding documents form the basis of American democracy. In particular, understanding why the Constitution was drafted the way it was compels people to dig even deeper.

Deceased author and former presidential speechwriter James C. Humes once said, "The art of communication is the language of leadership."[106] Good leaders are usually good communicators. President Trump frequently disrupts normal news cycles with tweets and statements that infuriate some and resonate with others. While most presidents grab attention with their pronouncements, Trump seems especially adept at marshaling attention.

His campaign slogan, "Make America Great Again," helped him win the presidency because it touched many. When Senator Bernie Sanders sought the presidency in 2016, he communicated a message to millennial voters and others of hope, emphasizing issues of importance to voters of all ages, but particularly to younger Americans disillusioned by politics. And Sanders came close to becoming the Democratic Party's nominee for president. Some leaders have a knack for speaking directly to voters, giving them hope for the future.

Citizenship and patriotism will grow if leaders communicate their importance. While many leaders have dedicated more of their attention to public policy matters than fostering citizenship and patriotism, perhaps the time has come to focus on the latter as a way of building a strong and enduring American democracy. When citizens lack understanding of their country and don't work to perpetuate the gifts of the democracy they've been handed, which others have sacrificed to preserve, there's no guarantee that the American system will be perpetuated.

CHAPTER 8

A LEGAL IMMIGRANT'S STORY

*"Patriotism is proud of a country's virtues
and eager to correct its deficiencies."*
–Sydney J. Harris

Between six hundred thousand and seven hundred thousand immigrants apply for American citizenship every year. They are required to pay a fee, meet age requirements, study for an oral immigration exam, interview with an immigration official and, if successful, participate in a swearing-in ceremony before a federal judge.[107] Applications for American citizenship have fluctuated between six hundred thousand and one million per year for the past fifty years, and anyone who hasn't observed an immigration ceremony should do so. Why?

Because there's joy in observing another human showing utter joy at becoming an American. They pledge their allegiance to their new country with sheer exuberance. The process of achieving citizenship is arduous. Some applicants struggle with the English language.

In 2012, the Nethercutt Foundation conducted a national survey of eight hundred Americans, asking three questions:

1. Should all federal public officials be knowledgeable about US history, government, economics, and foreign policy?

(Seventy-four percent said yes.)
2. Should American schools have civic learning as a core curriculum subject? (Eighty-five percent said yes.)
3. Should all Americans be able to pass the naturalization test that applicants for citizenship must pass to become citizens? (Sixty-seven percent said yes.)

That survey suggested that most Americans believe that knowing about America and the American system is important for our public officials, our schools, and us.

The process of immigration and the path to citizenship are carefully set forth on USA.gov. It starts with an application: applicants must have had a permanent resident green card for at least five years and must be at least eighteen years old. They must be able to read, write, and speak basic English and be of good moral character.

New citizens are encouraged to review the list of citizen rights and responsibilities provided. USCIS encourages all citizens to review, honor, and respect those rights and responsibilities, whether one is a naturalized or natural-born American citizen.

Going through the naturalization process means going through the ten steps: supporting and defending the Constitution; embracing the freedom to worship and express oneself; staying informed about community issues; participating in community affairs and the democratic process; respecting all laws as well as the rights, beliefs, and opinions of others; paying income taxes; appreciating one's right to a speedy and fair trial, the right to vote in elections, the right to apply for employment, and the right to seek public office; the responsibility to defend America if called upon to do so; the responsibility to serve on jury duty; and the right to pursue life, liberty, and happiness.

These rights and responsibilities form, in many cases, the basis for American patriotism. USCIS emphasizes that Americans share these citizenship rights and responsibilities in a country not bound by race or religion, but by "freedom, liberty, and equality." USCIS underscores that America has for decades welcomed people from across the globe, emphasizing that naturalized citizens are valuable and have bolstered American democracy. USCIS also acknowledges the importance of applying for American citizenship as an act of demonstrating commitment to the United States and the American form of government.[108]

A few questions on the naturalization test are:

- Name one of the two longest rivers in the US.
- The Federalist Papers supported the passage of the US Constitution. Name one of the writers.
- What is the rule of law?
- Under our Constitution, some powers belong to the states. What is one of the powers of the states?

Majda Ritchie, a twenty-six-year-old graduate of Gonzaga University and immigrant from Israel, is now an American citizen, having complied with all citizenship requirements and taken the Oath of Allegiance at a 2017 immigration ceremony. She's proud of her heritage and background. When I asked her about the naturalization process, she replied, "I'm originally from Israel. I wanted to become an American citizen after seeing and learning about the United States from the media. It illustrated American success, and I wanted that. At first, I came as a student and obtained a student visa. I planned to come here and go to school, and then go back to Israel. Even though Israel is a good country, we have a lot of problems. When I came to the United States, I wanted to be free and not be worried."

Freedom played a big part in Majda's wanting to become an American citizen. She chose the legal way to citizenship because she had the money for it. She didn't hire an immigration lawyer until the end of the process. The total cost was about four thousand dollars. It costs about six hundred dollars at every stage, payable to USCIS.

"I took the legal route because I didn't want to live in fear. The legal way is the right way to come into any country." She says she's not happy about all the illegal immigrants in the country, but she understands why someone would come into the United States without documentation — to help their family. "If you're poor and don't have money, but want to support your family, you enter illegally, and I totally understand that. I was fortunate enough to have the money to enter legally."

Majda got her green card as a student, then applied for American citizenship. The process was at times cumbersome (it took five years or so after she had completed her schooling, plus five years with a green card), and Majda even reached a point where she became discouraged and wanted to quit the process. "I felt like the country didn't want me, but I had made my life here," she said, and she continued to pursue citizenship. Majda married the love of her life in 2016. She wants children and wants to raise them in the United States. "I figure I belong here and you can't give up."

It was hard for her at first because she was in the country by herself — her family was back in Israel. As for their support, Majda says, "My dad was against it the whole way." Her mother, however, was in favor. "She believes in me, my dreams, and my goals." Her mom also came to the States for her wedding. Without her mother, Majda says, she would never have been able to come to America. Majda also has a younger sister and brother in Israel. Though she had been in the States for nine years and had a student visa for four years, she couldn't work. But eventually her status as a green card holder was changed and she became a permanent resident.

"I've always been patriotic," she said when I told her about writing this book. "I chose to come to this country, and I'm gonna fight for this country. It's more than just loving your country," she continued. "You have to be willing to defend it." She always believed the US was a great country and always thought of it as her home.

While preparing for the exit interview that would determine her citizenship status, Majda learned a lot about the United States and its history. She watched several television stations with differing points of view, feeling that acquiring several sides of a political discussion would prepare her to understand better the argument or discussion in question. She believes the strength of America lies in the ability of Americans to disagree about policy issues but still be patriotic. "The beauty of America is that we're all different and can learn from each other with the freedom to express different views," she says.

Majda represents a new wave of immigrants: tolerant of an open America, patriotic, aware of America's shortcomings, yet fiercely loyal to the country to which she pledges allegiance.

Legal immigration, while more onerous and costly than exceeding a legal stay in America or coming into the United States without proper documentation, is the preferable path. Legal immigrants who meet the citizenship obligations proceed under the color of law, free from the jeopardy that accompanies illegality and able to participate in the magic moment of being sworn in as a new American citizen with the same legal rights as any natural-born citizen.

Immigrants without proper documentation usually feel incomplete (see chapter 9), worrying that they'll be apprehended in the sweep of law enforcement. They are always on the lookout, even after years in the country. Those without documentation have to fear for their children, who could be "legal," but whose parents are not, thereby placing the family relationship in jeopardy. (DACA may be resolved by the time this book comes out.) Doing so places children in jeopardy and makes for insecure family relationships. Immigrants who follow the law and become citizens by following America's naturalization process needn't worry about deportation and the tearing apart of their families. Naturalized citizens have the right to vote and possess rights that are equal to natural-born citizens, something undocumented immigrants cannot claim.

Undocumented immigrants, sometimes using fake Social Security numbers,[109] are typically unable to build up a Social Security account; they cannot receive government benefits, and they receive no credit for taxes paid. They can be taken advantage of by unscrupulous employers, abused by coworkers and colleagues, and reported on by neighbors. In short, illegality breeds insecurity, while legality breeds justice and invocation of rights, conditions that help legal immigrants rest at east.

The swearing-in ceremony is the last effort an applicant must expend in order to achieve American citizenship. It is usually held in a public place or a federal courthouse. It is presided over by a federal judge. An American flag is often present. Children, spouses, other relatives, and friends may attend.

Cameras snap photos constantly. The USCIS has developed a video that runs continuously onstage, flashing patriotic slogans: photos of Abraham Lincoln, New York, the White House, the Capitol Building, Ellis Island, Niagara Falls, the Iwo Jima Memorial, Mt. Rushmore, and the Statue of Liberty. Interspersed are photos of the faces of immigrants and inspirational quotes like the following by applicants who achieved naturalization: "America has provided me a special opportunity: the freedom to choose my path." "Whatever I have dreamed America has always fulfilled."

"I am grateful to give back to my adopted country." "America is my peaceful refuge."

"Opportunities are only limited by your determination and faith."

"My fellow soldiers made me feel like I was an American. I obviously stand strong and Army proud as ever."

At a signing-in ceremony I attended in Spokane, Chief Judge of the US District Court for the Eastern District of Washington, Thomas O. Rice, presided. When he entered the room, all rose and remained standing through his welcoming remarks and the presentation of the colors by the Air Force ROTC Honor Guard. The National Anthem was sung a cappella. Judge Rice congratulated the new citizens and welcomed them to America. He acknowledged that September 17 was the 230th anniversary of the creation of the Constitution and that it was also Citizenship Day. He further noted that the Constitution was formed and signed by thirty-nine brave men, that it gives citizenship, and it requires allegiance to laws. He said that we are all citizens and that our system of government is "of, by, and for the people."

Justice Rice told the new citizens that they should participate in democracy, that the story of the United States of America is a story of immigrants, and that the new citizens shouldn't forget their heritage. He said that immigrant citizens bring skills and knowledge that are important to society and that the new citizens were now "neighbors, friends, and fellow citizens."

In a welcoming video, Justice Sotomayor greeted the new citizens and encouraged them to celebrate their citizenship at least once each year. She said that they had completed their "significant journey," some having fled oppression and intolerance to call America home. She acknowledged that it's never easy to adapt to a new country.

Justice Sotomayor stated that it is up to the immigrants to expand the promise of America. She urged them all to vote and express their views, to write their elected officials and volunteer, to serve on juries and meet the central obligations of citizenship. America has a history of collective success, she said, and diversity is "our greatest strength." She concluded by saying that if we honor it, "the promise of America will shine."

A USCIS officer moved for the admission of all 116 candidates for citizenship. After granting the motion, Judge Rice asked all applicants to raise their right hands while he administered the Oath of Citizenship. The applicants represented thirty-one countries. They renounced all allegiance and fidelity to any former state, prince, potentate, or other leader and swore to support and defend the Constitution against all enemies, foreign or domestic, and "bear true faith and allegiance to the same" (the Constitution), "including combatant and noncombatant services if called upon." Judge Rice affirmed that the new citizens took the obligation "freely, without any mental reservation or purpose of evasion," and swore on oath to God.

Congratulations and photos followed the swearing-in ceremony. The Daughters of the American Revolution (DAR) and the Sons of the American Revolution (SAR), both of which celebrate American heritage, took part in the ceremony, as did the Daughters of Union Veterans and Altrusa of Spokane. The Spokane County Auditor and the League of Women Voters helped with voter registration, and the new citizens eagerly signed up to vote. Citizen naturalization ceremonies are a long-standing and rich tradition in America. They happen regularly across the United States. The legal immigrant earns the right to be part of America with the same rights and responsibilities as those enjoyed by people born here.

Usually a sense of patriotism flows from the reality of achieving citizenship, and that patriotism translates to a love of country and a feeling of belonging. Those who choose the undocumented route cannot feel that sense of accomplishment, instead opting for whatever satisfaction comes from "outsmarting" authorities and avoiding US immigration authorities. It is obvious to anyone who attends a ceremony like the one in Spokane that those being sworn in are ecstatic that their long legal trek to becoming Americans has ended in citizenship. One can see and feel their patriotism.

CHAPTER 9

# AN UNDOCUMENTED IMMIGRANT'S STORY

*"True patriotism is a charity
so wide that it covers a nation."*
— Austin O'Malley

The difference between a documented and undocumented immigrant's story is one of connection with America. The naturalization applicant pays a fee, fills out paperwork, is the subject of a government official's interview, studies USCIS test questions to learn about America, and undergoes long waits that culminate in a ceremony celebrating the applicant's American citizenship. The undocumented immigrant does none of these tasks.

The main difference between the two can be summarized in one word: freedom. The documented immigrant need not worry about living in the country illegally, need not be fearful of getting caught, of being deported, or being convicted of a crime associated with undocumented status. The undocumented immigrant lives in fear — of getting caught, of getting crossways with law enforcement officials, of staying in the shadows of justice, of being exploited by others.

The story of undocumented immigration is one of not wanting your name revealed, of hiding from government officials, of concern for family members and friends who are also undocumented, of staying "underground" and in the shadows of the country. While their number has grown — to between ten and twelve million, as of November 2019[110] — they are looked at skeptically by many and suffer the disdain of those who are legal, documented immigrants, as well as by many who call America home. Children of undocumented immigrants suffer, too, always fearful that their family will be separated, their parents "found out." While many undocumented workers pay no federal or state tax, some do, but they're unable to participate in social programs offered by our government or to accumulate Social Security funds.

What follows is the story of an undocumented immigrant chronicling what he fears, the trials he has gone through, and how national identity — the patriotic and citizenship spirit — is different. This person didn't want to be identified by name, so we'll call him Kioko.

Kioko is originally from Kenya and came to the United States with his parents at the age of ten. After fifteen years in the States, Kioko remains undocumented. Kioko's parents are undocumented, too. Kioko is a Deferred Action for Childhood Arrivals (DACA) subject. DACA was introduced by President Obama in 2012 to allow some people who were brought to the US illegally as children to receive a renewable two-year period of deferred action from deportation and to be eligible for a work permit.

At time of publish, Kioko was attending a California university. He lives in fear — of being apprehended, of being found out, of being highlighted and used as an example . . . but he doesn't obsess over his status. He says you gain nothing as an undocumented immigrant. "For me, undocumented status has no advantages," he says. Stigma, lack of health insurance, and exploitation are all disadvantages to undocumented status. Kioko hopes that someday there will be an "opportunity to apply for citizenship," erasing the fundamental fears he feels at being an illegal immigrant, but right now he can only focus on what he can control, including his studies.

When asked why he didn't choose the documented, legal route, he says, "Such process wasn't extended to me." He's also concerned about how long it takes to become a citizen, citing that the federal immigration process through the USCIS in some cases is suffering a backlog extending to 2011. He knows of some applicants who have had to wait up to twenty-five years for citizenship. "Depending on where you come from, it could take decades to receive permanent legal residency or citizenship," he says. Thus, Kioko is critical of the refrain "Get in line, wait your turn, it's easy to get citizenship." He sees nothing easy about it.

He's done well as a student and is on the path to a PhD. He is thoughtful about the future and his place in it. Doubtful that he'd ever return to Kenya, Kioko also previously spent time at schools in Maryland and New York. He is receiving a quality education at a top California university. He wants to attend a top American law school and perhaps be a law professor someday.

But he's also concerned about being undocumented based on "recent decisions on immigration." His undocumented status is something he's learned to live with. He doesn't believe he should be upset about things he can't change, but he's still "vigilant about it, nevertheless."

Asked if he considers the States home and whether or not he feels patriotic about America, he says, "I don't know." He's gone through a lot in past years, and this is a country with which he's had a contentious relationship. He says there are many people who don't feel like they are part of the "American fabric."

Kioko agrees that Congress should pass comprehensive immigration measures but says that he and his colleagues don't have a lot of faith that Congress will act. He doesn't believe Congress will get anything done on the immigration issue.

He sees patriotism as having two competing definitions depending on one's perspective: one is uncritical of America, and the other is to call out when the American story has "gone wrong." He agrees with the latter and also with James Baldwin, the African American novelist and social critic who left America for Paris at age twenty-four and lived there most of his life until his death in 1987. The young illegal immigrant paraphrases Baldwin, saying, "I love America and that's why I criticize her." He doesn't think we should take this country as an "infallible creation," but that we should always call out problems and institutions that can be addressed, creating "a more perfect union." He doesn't speculate about what patriotism has been, but he focuses more on what it can mean: the ability to constructively criticize.

Immigrants who achieve citizenship status are often critical of those who enter America without documentation. The maxim of "closing the door once I've entered" seems all too prevalent among those who entered legally. One such view came from a person of Indian (from India) descent. Angry at the presence of so many "illegals" in America (he asserts the number is twenty-five million, not eleven million), he wants there to be a "time-out" for immigration or consideration of providing "illegals" with some form of citizenship. Supportive of the Trump administration's crackdown on immigration and supportive of DACA restrictions, he doesn't believe Congress will successfully address comprehensive immigration reform — to provide relief to those in America who are undocumented. Nor does he believe relief will be forthcoming for DACA subjects, whose status was threatened by President Trump.

Reform of America's immigration system is long overdue. President Trump has properly and legally placed the responsibility for legislation to address the DACA subjects on Congress. It is a legislative issue, one not fixable through presidential executive orders. The next chapter of this book contains a proposal for Congress to consider as it wrestles with the immigration issue.

Complicated and not easily solved, immigration reform is a critical issue to be solved in the twenty-first century. President Obama stated in a 2014 speech on immigration: "Today, our immigration system is broken, and everybody knows it. Families who enter our country the right way and play by the rules watch others flout the rules. Business owners who offer their workers good wages and benefits see the competition exploit undocumented immigrants by paying them less. All of us take offense to anyone who reaps the rewards of living in America without taking on the responsibilities of living in America. And undocumented immigrants who desperately want to embrace those responsibilities see little option but to remain in the shadows or risk their families being torn apart."[111]

Immigrants who are in the US legally tend to be among the most patriotic Americans, because they appreciate what the country has given them and they understand the system better than most natives. Immigrants here illegally may share the desire to show patriotism to their adopted country, but they can't. The system is broken, and it is time for the first major immigration reform since 1986. It is the patriotic thing to do.

CHAPTER 10

# HISTORY OF CITIZENSHIP AND A RECOMMENDATION

*"Citizenship is what makes a Republic; monarchies can get along without it."*
–Mark Twain

America has a history of adopting strict immigration legislation that nonetheless recognizes the enormous contributions immigrants have made and continue to make today to the country's economic and social fabric.

Usually federal judges, as they periodically preside over immigrant swearing-in ceremonies, extol the virtues of immigrants and the benefits they bring to American society, citing the importance of citizenship and fulfilling the rights and responsibilities of citizenship. Immigrants add diversity to our culture, offering new and often invigorating ways of thinking. They also often bring a work ethic not always found in native-born Americans. What follows is an examination of immigration laws that reflect the evolving attitudes about immigrants and their impact on American society. Note that Congress has often achieved bipartisan immigration legislation since America's founding in 1776.

In 1790, Congress adopted the US Naturalization Act. It established America's first comprehensive and uniform naturalization law. It provided citizenship for "free white persons" who had reached age twenty-one and resided in the States for at least two years provided they were of good moral character and swore allegiance to the Constitution. Children under twenty-one of naturalized citizens were also granted citizenship.[112]

In 1798, Congress passed what came to be known as the Alien and Sedition Acts, four laws that carried restrictive immigration enforcement provisions. They required a fourteen-year residence, contained broad presidential powers to restrain and deport immigrants if they were from countries with which the US was at war, and allowed the executive branch to deport individuals deemed "dangerous to the peace and safety of the US." These laws were eventually either repealed or expired naturally.[1-3]

The Immigration Act of 1864 created the position of commissioner of immigration within the State Department just as America was nearing the end of a bloody Civil War and months before the assassination of Abraham Lincoln, who signed the act into law. It further established that labor contracts entered into outside the United States were enforceable in US courts.[114]

In 1882, Congress enacted the first attempt at establishing broad immigration policy, the Immigration Act of 1882. It set a passenger tax of fifty cents for every non-citizen immigrant entering the country by ship from a foreign port. The law further created an immigration fund that the treasury secretary could use for immigration regulation. It also required the United States to screen arriving passengers and not admit "convicts, lunatics, idiots, or those unable to care for themselves without becoming a public charge."[115] The same year, Congress also passed the Chinese Exclusion Act,[116] America's first attempt to regulate immigration along racial lines. It suspended immigration for Chinese laborers for ten years but set November 17, 1880, as a cutoff date, allowing Chinese laborers who were already in the United States to remain, but excluding any Chinese laborers in the US after that date, allowing America to deport people of Chinese descent.

In 1888, the Scott Act[117] expanded on the Chinese Exclusion Act, forbidding Chinese who had left America from returning. In 1889, the US Supreme Court upheld the constitutionality of the Scott Act.

In 1889, President Benjamin Harrison, the twenty-third president, who served from 1889 to 1903, signed a law making it a federal misdemeanor to bring into the country or aid in bringing into the country any noncitizen unauthorized to enter. It also established a federal superintendent of immigration within the US Treasury Department.[118]

In 1892, Congress passed the Geary Act,[119] a law extending for an additional ten years the Chinese Exclusion Act and requiring those Chinese lawfully admitted previously to obtain certificates attesting to their lawful entry. The law also established a method of imposing imprisonment and one year of hard labor penalty on Chinese found guilty of entering the United States unlawfully, though the Supreme Court later struck down the hard labor provision as violating the Constitution's Fifth Amendment protections.

The 1917 Immigration Act expanded on the prior Chinese exclusions by establishing an "Asiatic Barred Zone,"[120] which included much of Asia and the Pacific Islands. Prohibitions under the law were expanded to prohibit the entry or reentry of anarchists, those not seeking special permission for reentry within one year, and those over age sixteen who couldn't read in their native languages.

In 1921, the Emergency Quota Act was passed by Congress.[121] It established the first "quota system" for immigrants, restricting the number of immigrants from countries to 3 percent of the number of residents from the same country living in the United States as of the 1910 census. This led to a dramatic reduction of immigrants from eastern and southern Europe and from non-European countries.

In 1924, Congress adopted the Johnson-Reed Act,[122] otherwise known as the 1924 National Origins Quota Act. It dropped the quota to 2 percent based on the 1890 census of foreign-born nationals. The law was criticized by some for using the 1890 census to discriminate against southern and eastern European immigrants who had come to the US in large numbers from 1890 to 1920. Supporters saw it as a necessary step to preserve the American identity. Students, certain Western Hemisphere nationals, certain professionals, and the wives and children of US citizens were exempted from the lower quotas.

In 1942, because of US labor shortages due to World War II, the United States and Mexico entered into the 1942 Bracero Agreement,[123] which allowed Mexican nationals to enter the country to serve as temporary agricultural workers. Congress extended the agreement in 1949 and 1951. It provided that US employers would pay these workers prevailing wages and provide transportation and living expenses for them. The agreement remained in force until 1964.

In 1943, the Magnuson Act[124] repealed the Chinese Exclusion Acts, thereby allowing Chinese nationals to become US citizens.

In 1945, the War Brides Act[125] allowed spouses and children of World War II veterans to be admitted into the United States.

President Truman signed the Displaced Persons Act in 1948,[126] allowing more than two hundred thousand persons displaced from their homelands by Nazi persecution to immigrate to the States. It further allowed up to fifteen thousand individuals residing in the US to adjust their statuses and become lawful permanent residents. President Truman was conflicted in signing the law, believing that it discriminated against Jewish displaced persons.

In 1952, the Immigration and Nationality Act,[127] otherwise known as the McCarran-Walter Act, was signed into law. It preserved the immigration quota system, consolidating several immigration laws, granting Asian countries immigration status, and establishing US consular officers eligibility to screen immigrants for admission to America. In 1953, Congress passed the Refugee Relief Act,[128] allowing 205,000 non-quota refugees fleeing persecution or expelled from their homes in Europe to be admitted to the US.

In 1962 President John F. Kennedy signed the Migration and Refugee Assistance Act of 1962.[129] It provided federal funds to assist those immigrants fleeing persecution in their home countries because of racial, political, or religious persecution. The law was intended to protect individuals fleeing persecution in Cuba and other countries under the influence of the Soviet Union.

In 1965, the Immigration and Nationality Act,[130] otherwise known as the Hart-Cellar Act, was adopted. It abolished the national quota system, replacing it with a system allowing immigrants to enter the country based on their relationship to a US citizen, a resident family member, or a US employer. A cap was put in place (raised to 120,000 in 1968 for Western Hemisphere residents), but there was no cap in the case of spouses, minor children, or parents. Immigrants from Western Hemisphere countries were also excluded from "preference categories."

The 1975 Indochina Migration and Refugee Assistance Act[131] expanded the definition of the 1962 act to include refugees fleeing from Cambodia and Vietnam.

The Immigration and Nationality Act Amendments of 1976[132] adopted the "preference categories" for Western Hemisphere immigrants set forth in the 1965 law.

The Refugee Act of 1980[133] established a new system for admitting refugees from foreign countries, allowing asylum for refugees outside their countries of origin unable or unwilling to return to that country for fear of persecution for racial, religious, social, or political preferences.

In 1986 Congress passed the Immigration Reform and Control Act.[134] The act provided enhanced penalties on employers hiring undocumented immigrants and increased border immigration enforcement staff. It also created two additional legal immigration programs: one allowing unauthorized aliens living in the United States since 1982 to "regularize" their statuses, and another permitting ninety-day agriculture workers to seek permanent resident status. About 2.7 million immigrants in the US used the law to become lawful permanent residents.

In 1988 the Anti-Drug Abuse Act was passed.[135] It added aggravated felony as a basis for deporting immigrants. It was initially limited to murder, weapons, and drug-trafficking offenses regardless of the sentence imposed or the time a legal resident had been in the States.

The 1990 Immigration Act[136] increased legal admissions, eased controls on temporary workers, and limited deportations. It expanded the scope of aggravated felonies to include political crimes of violence and eliminated discretionary relief for aggravated felons. It abolished judicial recommendations against deportation and terminated the discretion of sentencing judges to grant relief from deportation.

Congress enacted the Violent Crime Control and Law Enforcement Act in 1994.[137] It gave the US attorney general discretion to bypass deportation for certain alien aggravated felons, enhanced penalties for alien smuggling, and increased Border Patrol appropriations.

In 1996, the Antiterrorism and Effective Death Penalty Act was passed into law. It added more crimes to the aggravated felony definition and established expedited removal of immigrants without proper documentation or who were suspected of possessing fraudulent documents.

The Illegal Immigration Reform and Immigrant Responsibility Act was passed later in 1996.[138] It added new grounds of inadmissibility and deportability, expanded the list of crimes constituting an aggravated felony, created expedited removal procedures, and reduced judicial review of deportation cases. It expanded mandatory detention of immigrants previously convicted of certain crimes, increased the number of border agents, introduced new border control measures, and limited federal benefits for immigrants. It also increased penalties for illegal immigrants, imposed tougher requirements for asylum seekers, mandated a better entry/exit system for immigrants, and established a pilot program for employers and social service agencies to check immigrant status. The law also established state programs providing for immigration enforcement actions previously under federal jurisdiction.

In 1997 the Nicaraguan Adjustment and Central American Relief Act became law.[139] It provided deportation relief for immigrants from Nicaragua, Cuba, El Salvador, Guatemala, and certain former Soviet bloc countries.

The Haitian Refugee Immigration Fairness Act, providing similar assistance to Haitians who were present under the Nicaraguan law, followed it in 1998.[140]

On September 11, 2001, America was struck by three separate acts of terrorism. As a result, Congress passed the USA Patriot Act and President George W. Bush signed it into law.[141] It broadened terrorism acts as grounds for excluding aliens from entering the country and increased monitoring of foreign students, all intended to protect Americans from acts of terrorism by immigrants.

In 2002, the Enhanced Border Security and Visa Entry Reform Act was passed, requiring the development and implementation of an electronic data system while requiring an electronic entry/exit system.[142] As a result, the US-VISIT program was born to implement the system.

The year 2002 also brought into law the Homeland Security Act, creating the Department of Homeland Security (DHS) and placing all immigration services under DHS. Three new immigration agencies were created: Immigration and Customs Enforcement (ICE), US Citizenship and Immigration Services (USCIS), and Customs and Border Protection (CBP). The US Department of Justice's immigration services came under DHS jurisdiction as well.

In 2005, the Real ID Act became law.[143] It established guidelines for immigrant removal, expanded terrorism grounds for removal or deportation cases, and monitored border infrastructure measures. It required states to verify driver's license applications and identification cards used for federal identification purposes, barring the habeas corpus defenses to deportation and concentrating judicial review in appellate courts. The state driver's license requirements received pushback from state governments, which delayed implementation of the law.

In 2006, Congress enacted the Secure Fence Act[144] after the Senate failed to enact comprehensive immigration reform that had passed the House of Representatives in 2005. The Secure Fence Act required the construction of seven hundred miles of double-reinforced fencing along America's southern border in areas experiencing illegal immigration and increased drug trafficking. It also provided for enhanced enforcement technology that could control illegal immigration into the US.

The Migration Policy Institute (MPI) is led by two respected lawmakers, former US senator and energy secretary Spencer Abraham and former US representative and CEO of the Woodrow Wilson Center, Lee Hamilton.[145] The MPI analyzed current US immigration policy and compared major provisions of the 2013

Senate reform measure with Senate versions in 2006 and 2007 and the five subsequent House immigration bills. S. 744, titled the Senate Border Security, Economic Opportunity, and Immigration Modernization Act of 2013, was the last attempt by the Senate for comprehensive reform. It did not pass for lack of bipartisan support.

So, immigration has long been a major focus of legislators and the public, as the country has struggled with what its identity is, was, and should be. America has at times welcomed immigrants with open arms, and at other times has tried to close the doors. It's said that in America we're all immigrants.

Legal immigrants likely understand and embrace patriotism because they have a keen appreciation for the freedoms American citizenship confers. At numerous immigration ceremonies throughout the United States, federal judges routinely discuss the importance of citizenship — that is, voting in elections, volunteering in their communities, and participating in the community life where they reside. Judges also discuss citizens' rights and responsibilities. These rights and responsibilities must be fulfilled if America is to sustain our system of government over the long haul.

Comprehensive immigration reform is talked about every year by Congress and the president, but arriving at a plan that a majority can agree upon has proven elusive. The Deferred Action for Childhood Arrivals (DACA) program was implemented by executive order by President Obama in 2012 when Congress wouldn't (or couldn't) pass a DACA bill that satisfied Mr. Obama. His action was ill advised if not illegal,[146] and President Trump reversed the executive order and sought a permanent solution via Congress.[147] Congress passed a DACA law within six months. While many have criticized Mr. Trump's actions, he's correct that DACA was adopted temporarily, while no permanent solution currently exists. Some Democrats have criticized the Trump executive order overturning the

Obama executive order, yet no legislation has been introduced since 2012 to solve the DACA dilemma.[148]

Some Americans want more enforcement and others want a path to citizenship for immigrants who are undocumented. Yet, comprehensive reform must provide for more than these two positions. Some of the issues surrounding comprehensive immigration reform include increased border enforcement, verification requirements for employers, some legalization now for undocumented workers and undocumented students (many DACA children), and massive farm worker provisions. Whether to split up families in the course of immigration enforcement; H-1B visas (which allow employers to employ foreign workers in specialty occupations); wait-listing some applicants; and making the US immigration test more difficult are some of the considerations lawmakers ponder.

Perhaps an answer lies in improved relations with Mexico, from where many illegal immigrants commence their journey to the States. The Federation for American Immigration Reform[149] (FAIR), a nonprofit organization that seeks to reduce both legal and illegal immigration, lists seven principles of true comprehensive immigration reform:

1. Cut the numbers of admissions.
2. No amnesty or mass guest worker programs.
3. Protect wages and standards of living.
4. Do a major upgrade in interior enforcement led by strong employer penalties.
5. Stop special-interest asylum abuse.
6. Do an immigration time-out.
7. All should be equal under the law.

In 2013 the Judiciary Committee and Homeland Security Committee marked up (considered) five immigration reform bills in the House of Representatives: the Agricultural Guest Worker Act, the Border Security Results Act, the Legal Workforce Act, the SAFE Act, and the SKILLS Visa Act. None of these have received Senate consideration. The bills cover border security metrics and goals; border security plans; triggers; staffing and use of the National Guard; infrastructure improvements; fencing, technology, and equipment enhancements and emergency communications; federal lands provisions; state and local interagency collaboration; training; use of force; immigration ombudsman; detention and apprehension practices; overstays and oversight; among others.

Also included are general requirements; terms of conditional status; treatment for individuals apprehended in removal proceedings ordered removed or outside the country; fees and fines; eligibility for public benefits; extension of conditional status; application period; general qualifications; backing and adjustment of status for RPIs; diversity visa program; spouses and minor (under twenty-one) children of lawful permanent residents; other family preference categories; employment-based immigrants newly exempted from caps; other preference categories; employment and skills-based immigration; V visa; and discretion for immigration judges/DHS.

The Senate bill contains categories that cover integration policy and program coordination, public-private partnerships to support citizenship, grant programs, a naturalization process, and promoting naturalization.

The House bills have no such provisions. Gauging from the comprehensive nature of House and Senate legislation, immigration reform has many complicated aspects about which policy makers disagree, making such legislation difficult to enact. Both House and Senate versions cover employment verification and use of EEVs

(Employment Eligibility Verifications), worker protections, acceptable identity and work authorization documents, review of non-confirmations, protection against identity fraud and information sharing, use of driver's license information, penalties for hiring unauthorized workers, penalties for noncompliance with verification procedures, fraud-resistant Social Security cards and enhanced penalties for Social Security fraud, preemption, personnel and enhancements, worksite enforcement protections, and profiling.

Also included are provisions for exit system; authority of state and local law enforcement agencies; state, local, and federal cooperation; immigration enforcement personnel enhancements; and profiling. Other policy comparisons are conducted by MPI.

Comprehensive immigration reform should contain the following elements in order to pass Congress:

1. All entrants to America should be legal.
2. Border enforcement should be a priority (perhaps including a fence or other barrier).
3. DACA children should be covered under any comprehensive immigration reform, maybe with a special citizenship status. Perhaps the program should be curtailed in the future.
4. No amnesty.
5. High-tech visas should be available.
6. An E-verify program should be imposed.

President Trump's original immigration plan is contained in a campaign position paper.[150] The conservative CATO Institute supports it. The border wall was at the center of President Trump's immigration policy. Next is a mandatory e-verify requirement, and the third element is to end birthright citizenship. Ending birthright citizenship would likely require a constitutional amendment, which is never easy to accomplish. The fourth element is to end DACA, and the fifth calls for mandatory detention of all illegal immigrants. The sixth requires a "pause" in the issuance of new green cards to workers abroad so that employers will be forced to hire unemployed immigrants and natives.

Mr. Trump wants to increase the prevailing wage for H-1B employees, thereby reducing employer demand for them; force employers to hire American workers first; and raise the standards for refugee and asylum seekers to cut down on abuse and fraud. Per an American Action Forum study in 2015, President Trump said he believes that removing all illegal immigrants would save roughly $420 billion to $620 billion over twenty years,[151] though these estimates do not include negative economic effects or lost tax revenue from a resulting smaller economy.

Enacting the Trump administration's immigration priorities and assuring congressional adoption thereof will be difficult legislatively, but the time is right for immigration reform, especially as Mr. Trump "laid down the gauntlet" with his DACA action, challenging Congress to fix the problem with a law, not merely an impermanent, temporary executive order. He is likely underestimating the cost of deportation, especially if every deportable immigrant seeks a deportation hearing and an appeal. The cost of additional administrative judges, court costs, and detention costs pending a hearing could be high, offsetting deportation cost savings. The deportation process is dynamic, not static, thereby making cost estimates suspect.

In the meantime, at least eleven million undocumented immigrants residing in the US,[152] fearful of getting caught and unable to swear allegiance to America, thereby being American in residence only. About 10 percent of themare DACA subjects, essentially innocent victims of undocumented immigration by their parents.

*Saving Patriotism*  133

Having been brought into the country at a young age, they are now students or are gainfully employed. They love America and want to remain. Some accommodation should be made by Congress to accept them as American citizens, assuming they can pass background and civics tests to assure others that they know about America and can speak, write, read, and understand the English language. Having immigrants who love America will enhance patriotism. It always has.

CHAPTER 11

# A CALL TO PATRIOTIC ACTION

*"Patriotism is something that comes from within; it
will arise automatically when all citizens are treated equally
with love, harmony, and with an effort to reduce poverty,
starvation, caste inequality, and religious fanaticism."*
–Pravesh Jain

Many in the generation that will be America's future leaders are unpatriotic in the traditional sense. They think differently from their predecessors about "love of country" and "sacrifice." But they don't want their lifestyles to change either. Many have become used to America as they've known it — a land of privilege for most. "Sacrifice" traditionally means fighting for something precious and giving something up in the process. Usually it's a threat to something we hold dear, something we want to maintain — freedom, for example.

Many Americans don't know what it's like not to have the freedoms America offers. In the case of those who sacrificed for others, it means they gave up something (usually their safety) to benefit others (usually those they protected as they chose self-sacrifice over personal safety).

Most Congressional Medal of Honor winners and other military heroes will say they were "just doing their duty" when they risked personal safety to save others from harm. Their actions were decided in a split second for "patriotic impulses." That is, in retrospect, they and others saw their actions as patriotic because they sacrificed their own safety to benefit their fellow Americans. They usually didn't think of patriotism or being rewarded for their actions — they just acted out of impulse.

Medal of Honor winners are usually recognized in times of war on behalf of the branch of military they serve when they act heroically to help others survive. They're brave and courageous. They care less about themselves and more about their fellow men, all in the name of a patriotic spirit that places country and the welfare of others over self. They have a feeling that their sacrifice is expressed for a cause greater than themselves — the preservation of America.

It is the willingness to sacrifice that has sustained America and that will perpetuate the American system.

On the civilian side, there are fewer nationally recognized awards for heroism under pressure for the benefit of others. The Congressional Gold Medal, the Presidential Medal of Freedom, and the President's Award for Distinguished Federal Service are three awards that decorate civilians for bravery. They're typically issued for sustained meritorious service while in the service of the federal government. Most federal agencies offer similar awards for heroic accomplishments to their employees.

Of course, not all Americans can be medal winners, nor does the younger generation believe sacrifice in war is necessary to show their patriotism. Many younger Americans, for instance, are enlisting in programs such as the Peace Corps and AmeriCorps out of a sense of obligation to country and fellow man. So, for younger Americans, the future will have its moments of sacrifice in war by members of the military who deserve Medal of Honor recognition, but the vast majority of younger Americans won't be award candidates.

Many nevertheless love America, want to perpetuate the

American system, and are willing to sacrifice in ways other than joining the military. The key to the future of patriotic behavior lies in the younger generations' understanding that the American system is worth preserving and protecting. Perhaps all young people should be asked the following fundamental questions:

- What does it mean to be an American?
- What are you willing to do to preserve our rights and values?
- How far would you go to preserve the system?

How they answer will depend on whether they understand how our country works, what it stands for, and whether they appreciate the domestic and global responsibility it entails.

Millennial citizens and the generations that follow comprise the future of America. Instilling in them feelings of patriotism and enough love of country that they're willing to sacrifice their livelihoods and personal safety to preserve both of them is necessary for the future, too. They look at patriotism differently than their predecessors.

And society is changing. Whenever we see two people in a serious verbal quarrel, it's discomfiting. The same is true when public officials or officeholders "lose their cool" and get personal over some policy difference. Somehow we expect more of those who hold public positions. They're different from the rest of us. They've achieved more by being "certified" by the public as worthy of the offices they hold, so we hold them to a higher standard. A US representative has the title "Honorable" even after leaving office. Civility, treating others with respect, and discussing differences with dignity and without rudeness should be part of the public discourse.

And it doesn't stop with public officials — we should expect civility in all human relations. Civility, civic learning, good citizenship, and patriotism can be taught, emulated by others, and replicated. Most Americans copy behavior. That's why it's incumbent on citizens and officeholders alike to exhibit good behavior — because others watch and replicate what they see. When bad behavior is flashed on television, it's not long before a copycat acts likewise.

When we see parents reprimanding or abusing children verbally or physically, it's upsetting. When boyfriends or husbands argue in public with girlfriends or wives, it's repellant to observers. Wherever it occurs, incivility makes us uncomfortable. The same is true, or should be, when we see candidates personally attack one another in debates. Today, much of the civility we used to expect is lacking. Too many of us respond rudely to one another over the most minor incidents. Honking a horn to avoid a vehicle collision can draw a middle finger salute. Loud talking and obscenity-laced speech in public is more commonplace than ever. Disagreeing and being disagreeable now go hand in hand. And society is diminished as culture coarsens.

*Road and Travel Magazine* published a 2014 article about road rage citing a national survey confirming that 50 percent of road rage victims respond with road rage actions of their own — yelling, giving obscene hand gestures, horn honking.[153]

After the 9/11 tragedies, members of Congress were noticeably more polite to each other, exhibiting a desire to work together for America's common good following a national tragedy. The 9/11 experiences brought the world and Americans together for a shining moment of citizenship and civility. But it soon disappeared and partisan bickering returned.

Citizenship, civility, and patriotism need not be lost, especially if they're ingrained enough at an early age. Americans have gotten into the habit of being uncivil and unpatriotic. Americans reflect what they see at the highest levels of government. Watching politicians acting uncivil toward one another and viewing television programs that celebrate rudeness, intolerance, or lack of respect for another tend to make others follow suit. When the president of our country sends out uncivil tweets, news commentators and average Americans follow suit.

Some have concluded that America is doomed. Many Americans think not. America will survive, just as when foreign invasion was a threat — such as during WWII. Many Americans despaired, without food or a job, during the Great Depression. Today, creature comforts abound. There are more millionaires in America now than ever.[154] Most everyone carries a cell phone. Most every household has at least one television and one car. The future looks bright when economic growth picks up and joblessness decreases.

But what does the future look like for patriotism and citizenship as fewer Americans vote and polarization increases? As of 2019, millennials outnumbered baby boomers by about 72.1 million to about 71.6 million.[155]

And millennials are the key — these young people are the next generation of leaders. It is every older American's duty to groom them and prepare them for national service and leadership. A great example of this taking place is in the Mead School District in Spokane, Washington. The Senior-to-Senior Program allows a high school senior to interview a senior citizen so each can learn from the other. After meeting with students who had participated, it was clear the program is valuable. It's a surefire way to connect generations and prepare younger students for leadership as they understand more fully what their interviewees went through and what American history they've experienced. The program allows students to learn what senior citizens experienced, what they learned, and what wisdom they can pass along as they help younger Americans understand the sacrifices senior citizens have made to help America stay America.

What makes any nation great are leaders who effectively support the concepts that benefit the most people. In America's case, history has produced scores of leaders who became giants of their times. Senior citizens have real-life experiences to share, having witnessed some of the giants in action. The founders of our country were learned and principled men who had vision beyond their years. The leaders of today should not assume that the America they know today will include the principles of yesterday and that America will go on as she has for more than two centuries. Younger leaders will bring a host of new ideas forward to create a new America, born of similar principles but modernized to fit the needs of a younger generation.

Environmental protection, different forms of currency, computer technology, a greater interaction among nations of the world, less-strict borders, an influx of immigrants with modern ideas, and new faces of political leaders tearing down older ideologies will likely be the future. Such may be unsettling to older Americans, but the future belongs to the young.

And that's OK, because younger Americans will be the leaders of tomorrow — older Americans will be a memory. Young Americans today prefer politicians with a big heart for others; peace, not war; serving the less fortunate and protecting the environment, not just for Americans, but for the world. Millennial citizens are oftentimes much more magnanimous toward non-Americans, perhaps an attitude born of youth, not necessarily experience in life. One can be a principled conservative and still be compassionate for those who have little. That's the kind of patriotism that will serve all Americans well. It's also a blueprint for the fate that reveres the Constitution but makes it less narrow in its application. Following the Golden Rule is constitutionally consistent.

It seems that some Americans become more conservative with age, thereby reverting to a more traditional brand of patriotism. Magnanimity born of idealism shrinks some as Americans experience the ups and downs of life. As time goes by, Americans often become more protective of what they have and are less willing to give to others as they might have been in their youth. Oftentimes patriotic feelings increase for older Americans because the desire for America's positive future increases as Americans reach the end of life, wanting therefore to leave America materially better in the future.

The hope for perpetuation of the American system lies in the hands of our younger citizens, though. The future is theirs as they accept the responsibilities of leadership handed off by their predecessors.

Long-serving but now-deceased Arizona senator John McCain, no stranger to sacrifice in war, spoke of patriotism when he received the National Constitution Center's 2017 Liberty Medal at a ceremony in his honor on October 16, 2017, in Washington, DC. McCain stated, in pertinent part, "We believed in each other's patriotism [speaking of former senator and vice president Joe Biden] and the sincerity of each other's convictions. We believed in the institution we were privileged to serve in [the Senate]. We believed in our mutual responsibility to help make the place work and to cooperate in finding solutions to our country's problems. We believed in our country and in our country's indispensability to international peace and stability, and to the progress of humanity."

Quoting former president George H. W. Bush, McCain went on, "The most wondrous land on earth, indeed . . . What a privilege it is to serve this big, boisterous, brawling, intemperate, striving, daring, beautiful, bountiful, brave, magnificent country. With all our flaws, all our mistakes, with all the frailties of human nature as much on display as our virtues, with all the rancor of our politics, we are blessed. We are living in the land of the free, the land where anything is possible, the land of the immigrant's dream, the land with the storied past forgotten in the rush to the imagined future, the land that repairs and reinvents itself, the land where a person can escape the consequences of a self-centered youth and know the satisfaction of sacrificing for an ideal, the land where you can go from aimless rebellion to a noble cause . . . We are blessed, and we have been a blessing to humanity in turn.

"The international order we helped build from the ashes of world war [after WWII] and that we defend to this day has liberated more people from tyranny and poverty than ever before in history. This wondrous land has shared its treasures and ideals and shed the blood of its finest patriots to help make another, better world. And as we did so, we made our own civilization more just, freer, more accomplished ...

"We live in a land made of ideals, not blood and soil. We are the custodians of those ideals at home, and their champion abroad. We have done great good in the world. That leadership has had its costs, but we have become incomparably powerful and wealthy as we did. We have a moral obligation to continue in our just cause and we would bring more than shame upon ourselves if we don't. We will not thrive in a world where our leadership and ideals are absent. We wouldn't deserve to."[156]

McCain captured the spirit with which young citizens must lead America into the future. That future is one that will require an understanding and appreciation of civics, civility, and patriotism. And the patriotism is one that is traditional, born of experience and hardships, of sacrifice, and of commitment to an American ideal, taking into account the economic and social circumstances of all and recognizing that patriotism knows no race, social hardship, or economic circumstance.

The US Constitution has guided this country for more than two centuries and will continue to do so. All Americans should understand the essence and significance of the Constitution, and that will only happen with the restoration of civic learning in our classrooms.

According to the latest census, younger millennials are about 25 percent more likely to move from the city to suburbia than older millennials, who are 50 percent more likely to move there.[157] As the US struggles for better drainage from hurricanes and heavy rains in suburbia, millennial leaders will need to help meet the demand. Disdaining expensive housing, energy wastefulness, visual monotony, and the social conformity that often come with suburban development, the millennial generation will expect more. They'll figure out water management in rainy areas, energy efficiency through new technologies, and smaller-sized lots for houses. Cars and fuel consumption will be less attractive and necessary as electric cars and public transportation take their place. As they become more technologically sophisticated, drones will replace car travel. Self-driving cars will be more commonplace. More pedestrian-friendly neighborhoods will be prominent and accepted.

Policy makers will better understand global energy markets. Military options will likely be reduced as the new generation of leaders from foreign lands deals with America's new leaders. Wars in places such as Afghanistan and Iraq will be less frequent as millennials understand and learn from the futility of long-term conflicts that produce devastating consequences. Counterinsurgency, rather than unknown reactions that lead to war, will be prominent as Americans infiltrate foreign lands to understand the people's needs there before the outbreak of war.

Political skepticism will be more prominent as candidates strive for election. Television advertising, a staple of past elections, will likely be less prominent as other mediums take greater hold in politics. Many people get their news now from the internet. Three millennial-aged individuals in Colorado in 2016, while riding to the top of Pikes Peak, discussed how upset they were with the current political climate, declaring themselves "independents who used to be Republicans," perhaps signaling a political change. As the two major political parties wane in membership and independents grow, party labels will be less important as millennials vote for the person, not the party.

Isolationism will likely increase as millennial leaders focus their energies on the homeland. The election of Donald Trump as president convinces some that if he can get elected, any personality-driven individual of prominence can. That may result in a shift in political priorities as candidates with untraditional policies seek election. Such policies could include financial caution as younger leaders may eschew unfathomable national indebtedness and seek to protect social programs to cover the needy in American society. Remote working will replace "coming to the office every day." With the status of technology, remoteness will be more accepted, expenditures on gas for cars will be reduced, and personal interaction will be at a premium.

Cash will be less important as cryptocurrencies and online payments for goods become the norm. Paper copies will likely be obsolete as millennials cut down on clutter.

The owner of one of the oldest businesses in Italy, a ceramics company called Grazia Deruta that dates from 1548, struggles for business because younger generations would rather possess ceramic dishes from China than the real thing. Baby boomer friends of mine say that their millennial children do not desire their parents' antique furniture. In Florence, Italy, crafts that have been in demand for generations are losing business because younger people couldn't care less for such handiwork.[158]

Yes, the world will change politically, socially, culturally, and economically as tomorrow's leaders gain power and influence. Yet, millennials had best not dismiss US history, capitalism, and free markets, understanding how government works, and learning foreign policy principles. There are valuable lessons for leaders of tomorrow to learn. They should start with the basics of civics and arm themselves with knowledge that prepares them to call on lessons of history in their decision-making. World history is replete with examples of lessons of the past not learned.

Today's communication affords the quick and easy transmission of information. With some five hundred cable channels (not all news channels), all of them vying for business, citizens don't know what to believe, so the national news channels should always strive to be truthful. If they are, the world the baby boomers leave behind will be one the next generation can develop under the Constitution.

Patriotism is changing as younger Americans see the futility of war and waste of mass death, as well as the advancement of the computer. They seek other ways to be patriotic, ways that minimize conflict and fighting, ways that affirm individual and national goodness. Theirs may be the way of the future, but the danger in their ways lies in the desire to become a global community without boundaries or distinction.

The world is made up of human beings everywhere, with similar human wants and desires — and not always for the public good. The danger in their thinking is that it could result in America's changing in the future to become less "American" and more global, where citizens don't identify with any country or system of government. In such a world, the traditional patriotism that distinguishes American goodness from other, lesser governmental systems that don't include compassion can be lost. That's why American identity is important to maintain, because America is "different" and "better" than competing governmental systems (e.g., communism, pure socialism), where goodness and magnanimity are not as evident as national values.

A seventy-four-year-old friend of mine once said to me, "I wish I could live to be a hundred and fifty years old, just to observe what the future looks like." According to futurists, the future world will look different from what it looks like today. Some have predicted a ten-year transition from the internet to the brain-net, where thoughts and emotions, feelings and memory will be transmitted instantly across the planet, and the decoding of memory and emotions through computers will occur.[159] Printers that are 3D capable will be able to print clothing at low cost, human organs will be reproduced using stem cells, and disease will be more easily eradicated.

All this will further shrink the world, with the potential to obliterate national boundaries by integrating all peoples into one world, thereby necessitating a patriotism that distinguishes America from other nations. This will be necessary to perpetuate the "goodness" of which Senator McCain eloquently spoke that has brought prosperity and benefit to many humans.

The world needs a beneficent nation, if for nothing else than to illustrate what goodness looks like. It is politically expedient to affect others through competitive government, trade imbalance, or military might. The world, therefore, needs a nation that will step in when necessary to maintain order and prevent one nation from dominating another, whether a country tries this out of self-interest or because of a dictator's desire for power.

The United States, possessed of military might and economic success, is that nation. That's why perpetuation of democracy and freedom, no matter how technology changes or society modernizes, is necessary. That, in turn, means that patriotism will always be necessary. The perpetuation of the American way depends on patriotism, and patriotism will become a thing of the past unless we demand a return of civic learning to our classrooms.

An understanding by all Americans of American history, government, economics, and political science is essential to our future.

# Conclusion

This book about patriotism serves less as a "how to" and more as a "what is," defining patriotism and offering perspectives on the topic, as well as historical references.

Patriotism is definitely country oriented, but it's also deeply personal. It begs the question of how a person can be patriotic to their country without joining the military and fighting for American supremacy in the world. Of course, it's possible to be patriotic without defending America with arms or being elected to public office. Personal patriotism can be as simple as understanding how government works, being knowledgeable of current affairs, or even volunteering to enhance a community or improve someone else's life. The beauty of America emanates from the freedoms Americans enjoy.

American patriotism makes the United States stronger. Knowing about America makes us all better Americans. Understanding how the institutions of government work is an essential part of civic learning and of citizenship.

There are three keys to enhanced patriotism: schools, leaders, and the media:

1. SCHOOLS: Schools have the greatest access to young people — the next generation of leaders. If schoolteachers and

professors embrace patriotism, encouraging their students to study and know how the American system works by being steeped in current and past affairs of state, they can be future leaders who have a background in civic learning and learn how to be a better citizen. The best teachers make a subject exciting to their students. There's plenty of drama in US history to make it exciting. Awards could be given for outstanding patriotic scholarship.
2. LEADERS: Political leaders and other public officials have loud and effective voices with which they can spread information about the importance of patriotism and civics. Passing laws or regulations that bolster patriotism will impact the public discussion surrounding civic learning. Being examples through their actions could spur others to replicate the model made by public servants.
3. MEDIA: Those who control the news media, podcasts, radio, television, publications, and cable hold vast power over what consumers are exposed to. If media outlets of all kinds would emphasize the importance of patriotism at some point each day, the public would get the message and civic learning would be enhanced. The media should cover acts of public officials who seek to enhance patriotism and pay attention to schools and teachers who teach it.

The civically ignorant are not well-rounded. Patriotism requires a commitment, but it's not entirely unilateral. The commitment must come from the citizen, of course, but it must be encouraged by others: public officials, teachers or school administrators, corporate or business leaders, or media figures all working together can impact America for the better.

And democracy is at a crossroads. Some have opined that if young people don't learn civics now — this generation — they'll never learn it. There are numerous groups that support civic learning, and they should be called upon for their expertise. The previously mentioned Association of Former Members of Congress has a civics focus that touches all former members of Congress. Civic learning is nonpartisan, too. When I submitted an article to the *Seattle Times* calling for more civic learning, thirteen other former members of Congress, including Republicans, Democrats, liberals, conservatives, senators, and representatives from across America, joined willingly, saying that they supported anything stressing the importance of civics.

The Nethercutt Civics Foundation boasts a bipartisan advisory group consisting of four former members of Congress, a former ambassador, a college president, the owner of a speakers' bureau, a former professional baseball player, recent students, and numerous business experts. I invite you to spend some time on the site (www.nethercuttcivicsfoundation.org) and get involved. Patriotism's time has come. Now is the time to stress it.

# ENDNOTES

1. Schrein, C. M. (2015) "Lucy: A marvelous specimen." *Nature Education Knowledge. 6*(7):2.
2. Zachos, Elaina. "3.6-Million-Year-Old Human Ancestor Unveiled to Public." *National Geographic*, last modified December 6, 2017. https://www.nationalgeographic.com/news/2017/12/million-year-old-human-ancestor-unveiled-to-public-spd/.
3. Shreeve, Jamie. "Oldest Skeleton of Human Ancestor Found." *National Geographic*. Oct. 2009. https://www.nationalgeographic.com/science/2009/10/oldest-skeleton-human-ancestor-found-ardipithecus/.
4. "Watch American University students fail to name single U.S. senator." Yahoo News. March 27, 2014. https://news.yahoo.com/college-students-fail-us-senator-142856377.html/.
5. Jones, Sasha; Education Week Library. "Data: Most States Require History, But Not Civics." Education Week, Center for American Progress. Oct. 28, 2018. Vol. 38, no.10. https://www.edweek.org/ew/section/multimedia/data-most-states-require-history-but-not.html/.
6. Bowman, Karlyn; O'Neil, Eleanor. "AEI Public Opinion Study: Polls on patriotism, 2017." American Enterprise Institute. https://www.aei.org/research-products/report/aei-public-opinion-study-polls-on-patriotism-2017/.
7. Samuelson, Robert J. "Americans are historically unhappy. But there is a lesson to learn here." *Washington Post*. July 3, 2020. https://www.washingtonpost.com/opinions/americans-are-historically-unhappy-but-theres-a-lesson-to-learn-here/2020/07/03/4b882c7e-bbbb-11ea-8cf5-9c1b8d7f84c6_story.html/.
8. Romano, Andrew. "How Ignorant Are Americans?" *Newsweek*. Mar. 20, 2011. https://www.newsweek.com/how-ignorant-are-americans-66053/.
9. Woodard, Colin. "Half of Americans Don't Vote. What Are They Thinking?" *Politico*. Feb. 19, 2020. https://www.politico.com/news/magazine/2020/02/19/knight-nonvoter-study-decoding-2020-election-wild-card-115796/.

10. "Civics: 2018 Civics Results." National Center for Education Statistics. https://nces.ed.gov/nationsreportcard/civics/.

11. "Civics Framework for the 2018 National Assessment of Educational Progress." National Assessment Governing Board; U.S. Department of Education. 2018. https://www.nagb.gov/content/nagb/assets/documents/publications/frameworks/civics/2018-civics-framework.pdf/.

12. "Political Polarization." Pew Research Center. 2020. https://www.pewresearch.org/topics/political-polarization/.

13. Saad, Lydia. "Americans' Take on the U.S. Is Improved, but Still Mixed." Gallup. Jan. 27, 2020. https://news.gallup.com/poll/284033/americans-improved-mixed.aspx/.

14. Shearer, Elisa; Gottfried, Jeffrey. "Half of those who aren't learning about the election feel their vote doesn't matter." Pew Research Center. March 4, 2016. https://www.pewresearch.org/fact-tank/2016/03/04/half-of-those-who-arent-learning-about-the-election-feel-their-vote-doesnt-matter/.

15. History.com editors. "Marshall Plan." History. Original: Dec 16, 2009; Updated: June 5, 2020. https://www.history.com/topics/world-war-ii/marshall-plan-1.

16. "George C. Marshall Timeline & Chronology." The George C. Marshall Foundation. https://www.marshallfoundation.org/marshall/timeline-chronology/.

17. Lange, Katie. "9 Notable Presidents Who Served." U.S. Department of Defense. Feb. 18, 2019. https://www.defense.gov/Explore/Features/Story/Article/1757274/9-notable-presidents-who-served/.

18. Bureau of Near Eastern Affairs. "U.S. Relations With Iraq Bilateral Relations Fact Sheet." U.S. Department of State. Nov. 13, 2019. https://www.state.gov/u-s-relations-with-iraq/.

19. "U.S. Relations With Afghanistan Bilateral Relations Fact Sheet." Bureau of South and Central Asian Affairs. July 8, 2019. https://www.state.gov/u-s-relations-with-afghanistan/.

20. "Bush: WWII Memorial a 'fitting tribute.'" CNN. May 30, 2004. http://edition.cnn.com/2004/US/05/29/bush.transcript/index.html/.

21. Burke, Matthew M. "The story of an iconic statue made from an iconic photograph taken at Iwo Jima." *Stars and Stripes.* Mar. 27, 2020. https://www.stripes.com/news/us/the-story-of-an-iconic-statue-made-from-an-iconic-photograph-taken-at-iwo-jima-1.624015/.

22. Heimlich, Russell. "A Nation of Flag Wavers." Pew Research Center. June 22, 2011. https://www.pewresearch.org/fact-tank/2011/06/22/a-nation-of-flag-

wavers/.

23. "Washington Crossing the Delaware." Metropolitan Museum of Art. https:// www.metmuseum.org/art/collection/search/11417/.

24. History.com editors. "Battles of Trenton and Princeton." History. Original: Nov. 9, 2009; updated Feb. 6, 2020. https://www.history.com/topics/american-revolution/battles-of-trenton-and-princeton#:~:text=General%20George%20Washington's%20army%20crossed,of%20Hessian%20mercenaries%20before%20withdrawing/.

25. "This Day in History; Dec. 19, 1776; Thomas Paine publishes 'The American Crisis.'" History. https://www.history.com/this-day-in-history/thomas-paine-publishes-american-crisis#:~:text=%22These%20are%20the%20times%20that,thanks%20of%20man%20and%20woman/.

26. "Quotations by Hubert Humphrey." WIST (Wish I'd Said That). https://wist.info/author/humphrey-hubert/.

27. "This Day in History; July 30, 1956; President Eisenhower signs 'In God We Trust' into law." History. https://www.history.com/this-day-in-history/president-eisenhower-signs-in-god-we-trust-into-law/.

28. Sawe, Benjamin Elisha. "List of State Mottos." World Atlas. April 11, 2019. https://www.worldatlas.com/articles/list-of-state-mottos.html/.

29. "First Inaugural Address of Ronald Reagan; Jan. 20, 1981." Yale Law School Lillian Goldman Law Library. https://avalon.law.yale.edu/20th_century/reagan1.asp/.

30. Washington Library; Center for Digital History; Quotes. https://www.mountvernon.org/library/digitalhistory/quotes/article/citizens-by-birth-or-choice-of-a-common-country-that-country-has-a-right-to-concentrate-your-affections-the-name-of-american-which-belongs-to-you-in-your-national-capacity-must-always-exalt-the-just-pride-of-patriotism-more-than-any-appellation-derived-fr/.

31. Andrews, Evan. "Patrick Henry's 'Liberty or Death' Speech; On the anniversary of Patrick Henry's stirring words at the 1775 Virginia Convention, take a look back at the speech that included the famous line, 'Give me liberty or give me death!'" History. Original: March 22, 2015; Updated: Aug. 22, 2018. https://www.history.com/news/patrick-henrys-liberty-or-death-speech-240-years-ago/.

32. "Today in History - May 20, 1736; Patrick Henry, Orator of Liberty." Library of Congress. https://www.loc.gov/item/today-in-history/may-29/.

33. "The Gettysburg Address." Cornell University. 2013 Division of Rare &

Manuscript Collections. https://rmc.library.cornell.edu/gettysburg/good_cause/transcript.htm/.

34. "Lincoln Memorial Inscriptions." National Park Services. https://www.nps.gov/linc/learn/historyculture/inscriptions.htm#:~:text=In%20addition%20to%20the%20inscription,walls%20of%20the%20Lincoln%20memorial.&text=Lincoln%20delivered%20the%20Gettysburg%20Address,for%20the%20Soldiers'%20National%20Cemetery/.

35. Freidel, Frank; Sidey, Hugh. "The Presidents of the United States of America." 2006. The White House Historical Association. https://www.whitehouse.gov/about-the-white-house/presidents/theodore-roosevelt/.

36. Klein, Christopher. "When Teddy Roosevelt Was Shot in 1912, a Speech May Have Saved His Life; It takes more than that to kill a Bull Moose." History. Original: Oct. 12, 2012; Updated July 21, 2019. https://www.history.com/news/shot-in-the-chest-100-years-ago-teddy-roosevelt-kept-on-talking/.

37. "This day in history; November 7, 1944; FDR wins unprecedented fourth term." History. https://www.history.com/this-day-in-history/fdr-wins-unprecedented-fourth-term/.

38. "President Roosevelt's Inaugural Address. March 4, 1933." PBS. https://www.pbs.org/newshour/spc/character/links/roosevelt_speech.html/.

39. Chan, Melissa. "'A Date Which Will Live in Infamy.' Read President Roosevelt's Pearl Harbor Address." *Time*. Originally published Dec. 7, 2016; updated Dec. 6, 2018. https://time.com/4593483/pearl-harbor-franklin-roosevelt-infamy-speech-attack/.

40. "John F. Kennedy's Inaugural Address." John F. Kennedy Presidential Library and Museum. https://www.jfklibrary.org/learn/education/teachers/curricular-resources/elementary-school-curricular-resources/ask-not-what-your-country-can-do-for-you/.

41. "Civil Rights Movement." John F. Kennedy Presidential Library and Museum. https://www.jfklibrary.org/learn/about-jfk/jfk-in-history/civil-rights-movement/.

42. "Inaugural Address of President John F. Kennedy; January 20, 1961." John F. Kennedy Presidential Library and Museum. https://www.jfklibrary.org/archives/other-resources/john-f-kennedy-speeches/inaugural-address-19610120#:~:text=Let%20every%20nation%20know%2C%20whether,and%20the%20 success%20of%20liberty/.

43. "This day in history; April 11, 1951; President Truman relieves General MacArthur of duties in Korea." History. https://www.history.com/this-day-in-

history/truman-relieves-macarthur-of-duties-in-korea/.

44. "Duty, honor, country address at West Point by General Douglas MacArthur; 1962." CommonLit. https://www.commonlit.org/texts/duty-honor-country-address-at-west-point/.

45. History.com editors. "Douglas MacArthur." History. Original: Oct. 29, 2009; updated June 7, 2019. https://www.history.com/topics/world-war-ii/douglas-macarthur/.

46. "'I Have a Dream,' Address Delivered at the March on Washington for Jobs and Freedom; by Martin Luther King, Jr. Aug. 28, 1963." Stanford University. https://kinginstitute.stanford.edu/king-papers/documents/i-have-dream-address-delivered-march-washington-jobs-and-freedom/.

47. Biography.com editors. "James Earl Ray Biography (1928-1998)." Biography. Original: April 22, 2015; updated Jan. 17, 2020. https://www.biography.com/crime-figure/james-earl-ray#:~:text=A%20confirmed%20racist%20and%20small,prison%20on%20April%2023%2C%201998/.

48. "Farewell Address to the Nation by Ronald Reagan; Jan. 11, 1989." Reagan Foundation. https://www.reaganfoundation.org/ronald-reagan/reagan-quotes-speeches/farewell-address-to-the-nation-2/.

49. "Reagan quotes and speeches." Reagan Foundation. https://www.reaganfoundation.org/ronald-reagan/reagan-quotes-speeches/?topic=All&search=tax&sort=/.

50. "This day in history; March 29, 1973. U.S. withdraws from Vietnam." History. https:// www.history.com/this-day-in-history/u-s-withdraws-from-vietnam/.

51. Puddington, Arch; Roylance, Tyler. "Anxious Dictators, Wavering Democracies: Global Freedom under Pressure." 2016. Freedom House. https://freedomhouse.org/sites/ default/files/FH_FITW_Report_2016.pdf/.

52. Wallace, Gregory. "Voter turnout at 20-year low in 2016." CNN. Updated Nov. 30, 2016. https://www.cnn.com/2016/11/11/politics/popular-vote-turnout-2016/index.html/.

53. Shepard, Steven. "Gun control support surges in polls." *Politico*. Feb. 28, 2018. https://www.politico.com/story/2018/02/28/gun-control-polling-parkland-430099/.

54. Reilly, Katie. "A generational gap in American patriotism." Pew Research Center." July 3, 2013. https://www.pewresearch.org/fact-tank/2013/07/03/a-generational-gap-in-american-patriotism/.

55. Morales, Lamar. "One in Three Americans 'Extremely Patriotic';

Republicans, conservatives, and seniors most likely to say so." Gallup. July 2, 2010. https://news.gallup.com/poll/141110/One-Three-Americans-Extremely-Patriotic.aspx/.

56. Heimlich, Russell. "Generational Divide Over American Exceptionalism." Pew Research Center. Nov. 18, 2011. https://www.pewresearch.org/fact-tank/2011/11/18/generational-divide-over-american-exceptionalism/.

57. "The Military-Civilian Gap: Fewer Family Connections." Pew Research Center. Nov. 23, 2011. https://www.pewsocialtrends.org/2011/11/23/the-military-civilian-gap-fewer-family-connections/.

58. "Employee job satisfaction and engagement; revitalizing a changing workforce." Society for Human Resource Management. 2016. https://www.shrm.org/hr-today/trends-and-forecasting/research-and-surveys/Documents/2016-Employee-Job-Satisfaction-and-Engagement-Report.pdf/.

59. Gillespie, Mark. "Americans Feeling More Patriotic This Independence Day; Eight in 10 will display an American flag on the Fourth of July." Gallup. July 3, 2002. https://news.gallup.com/poll/6337/americans-feeling-more-patriotic-independence-day.aspx/.

60. Stone, Andrea. "'Civic generation' rolls up sleeves in record numbers." *USA Today*. April 9, 2009. http://usatoday30.usatoday.com/news/sharing/2009-04-13-millenial_N.htm/.

61. Wimmer, Andreas. "Why Nationalism Works And Why It Isn't Going Away." *Foreign Affairs*. March/April 2019. https://www.foreignaffairs.com/articles/world/2019-02-12/why-nationalism-works/.

62. "Dissent is the highest form of patriotism (Spurious Quotation)." Thomas Jefferson Encyclopedia. https://www.monticello.org/site/research-and-collections/dissent-highest-form-patriotism-spurious-quotation/.

63. "Constitution Day." United States Senate. https://www.senate.gov/artandhistory/history/common/generic/ConstitutionDay.htm/.

64. Tourtellot, Arthur Bernon. "We Mutually Pledge To Each Other Our Lives, Our Fortunes And Our Sacred Honor." *American Heritage*. December 1962. Vol. 14, No. 1. https:// www.americanheritage.com/we-mutually-pledge-each-other-our-lives-our-fortunes-and-our-sacred-honor/.

65. Biography.com editors. "John Marshall Biography." Biography. https://www.biography.com/political-figure/john-marshall/.

66. "Civil War Casualties." American Battlefield Trust. https://www.battlefields.org/learn/articles/civil-war-casualties/.

67. History.com editors. "Abraham Lincoln's Assassination." Original: Oct.

27, 2009; updated April 13, 2020. https://www.history.com/topics/american-civil-war/abraham-lincoln-assassination#:~:text=On%20the%20evening%20of%20April,at%20Appomattox%20Court%20House%2C%20Virginia%2C/.

68. Little, Becky. "How Martin Luther King Jr. Took Inspiration From Gandhi on Nonviolence; The civil rights leader realized the power in Gandhi's approach to standing up to oppression with 'truth-force.'" Biography. Original: Jan. 11, 2019; updated June 18, 2020. https://www.biography.com/news/martin-luther-king-jr-gandhi-nonviolence-inspiration#:~:text=Luther%20King%20Jr.-,Took%20Inspiration%20From%20Gandhi%20on%20Nonviolence,with%20%22truth%2Dforce.%22&text=Mahatma%20Gandhi%20inspired%20people%20all,leaders%2C%20Martin%20Luth er%20King%20Jr./.

69. "March on Washington for Jobs and Freedom." Stanford University; The Martin Luther King, Jr. Research and Education Institute. https://kinginstitute.stanford.edu/encyclopedia/march-washington-jobs-and-freedom/.

70. History.com editors. "Compromise of 1877." History. https://www.history.com/topics/us-presidents/compromise-of-1877/.

71. History.com editors. "Plessy v. Ferguson." History. Original: Oct. 29, 2009; updated Feb, 21, 2020. https://www.history.com/topics/black-history/plessy-v-ferguson#:~:text=Sources-,Plessy%20v.,in%20a%20car%20for%20blacks/.

72. History.com editors. "Domino Theory." History. Original: Nov. 9, 2009; updated Aug. 24, 2018. https://www.history.com/topics/cold-war/domino-theory/.

73. "Vietnam War U.S. Military Fatal Casualty Statistics." Electronic Records Reference Report. Archives.gov. Page last reviewed April 30, 2019. https://www.archives.gov/research/military/ vietnam-war/casualty-statistics/.

74. "Vietnam War Facts, information, and articles about the Vietnam War." Historynet. https://www.historynet.com/vietnam-war/.

75. History.com editors. "This day in history; March 29, 1973; U.S. withdraws from Vietnam." History. Originally published Nov. 24, 2009; updated March 26, 2020. https://www.history.com/this-day-in-history/u-s-withdraws-from-vietnam/.

76. U.S. News Staff. "Pentagon Papers: Secret Decisions That Altered the Vietnam War; The impact of the Pentagon's analysis of the government's policy-making processes on Vietnam extends far beyond the war itself, this 1971 U.S. News article indicates." *U.S. News & World Report*. June 13, 2016. https://www.usnews.com/news/articles/2016-06-13/pentagon-papers-secret-decisions-that-altered-the-vietnam-war/.

77. Lange, Allison. "Suffragists Unite: National American Woman Suffrage

Association." National Women's History Museum. Fall 2015. http://www.crusadeforthevote.org/nawsa-united/.

78. Costello, Matthew. "Picketing the White House; the suffragist movement during the great war." The White House Historical Association. April 14, 2017. https://www.whitehousehistory.org/picketing-the-white-house/.

79. McGreevy, Nora. "In 1872, Susan B. Anthony Was Arrested for Voting 'Unlawfully'; President Donald Trump posthumously pardoned the pioneering activist on the 100th anniversary of women's suffrage." *Smithsonian Magazine.* Aug. 18, 2020. https://www.smithsonianmag.com/smart-news/why-susan-b-anthony-was-arrested-1872-180975587/.

80. Lehman, Godfrey D. "Susan B. Anthony Cast Her Ballot For Ulysses S. Grant. For this crime, she was arrested, held, indicted, and put on trial. Judge Hunt presided." *American Heritage.* December 1985. Vol. 37, no. 1. https://www.americanheritage.com/susan-b-anthony-cast-her-ballot-ulysses-s-grant/.

81. History.com editors. "This day in history; March 31, Abigail Adams urges husband to 'remember the ladies.'" History. March 30, 2020. https://www.history.com/this-day-in-history/abigail-adams-urges-husband-to-remember-the-ladies/.

82. History.com editors. "Prohibition." History. Originally Published Oct. 29, 2009; updated Jan. 27, 2020. https://www.history.com/topics/roaring-twenties/prohibition/.

83. Blakemore, Erin. "How the Black Power Protest at the 1968 Olympics Killed Careers; When Tommie Smith and John Carlos raised their fists in protest at the 1968 Summer Games, Australian runner Peter Norman stood by them. It lost him his career." History. Originally published Feb. 22, 2018; updated Oct. 19, 2018. https://www.history.com/news/1968-mexico-city-olympics-black-power-protest-backlash/.

84. Ibid.

85. Black Lives Matter. https://blacklivesmatter.com/about/.

86. Moody, Chris. "O'Malley apologizes for saying 'all lives matter' at liberal conference." CNN. July 19, 2015. https://www.cnn.com/2015/07/18/politics/martin-omalley-all-lives-matter/ index.html/.

87. "Whose Heritage? Public Symbols of the Confederacy." Southern Poverty Law Center. Feb. 1, 2019. https://www.splcenter.org/20190201/whose-heritage-public-symbols-confederacy/.

88. Pietsch, Bryan. "Princeton Will Remove Woodrow Wilson's Name From

School." *The New York Times*. June 27, 2020. https://www.nytimes.com/2020/06/27/nyregion/princeton-university-woodrow-wilson.html/.

89. Newman, Andy; Wang, Vivian. "Calhoun Who? Yale Drops Name of Slavery Advocate for Computer Pioneer." *The New York Times*. Sept. 3, 2017. https://www.nytimes.com/2017/09/03/nyregion/yale-calhoun-college-grace-hopper.html/.

90. Johnson, Martenzie; The Undefeated. "Colin Kaepernick's parents break silence: 'We absolutely do support him.'" ESPN. Dec. 10, 2016. https://www.espn.com/nfl/story/_/id/18247113/colin-kaepernick-parents-break-silence-speak-support-criticized-quarterback/.

91. Norris, Luke. "Colin Kaepernick's Birth Mother Supports His Cause But Has Scolded Him on Twitter on Numerous Occasions." Sportscasting. June 23, 2020. https://www.sportscasting.com/colin-kaepernicks-birth-mother-supports-his-cause-but-has-scolded-him-on-twitter-on-numerous-occasions/.

92. "Independent States in the World; fact sheet." U.S. Department of State. Bureau of Intelligence and Research. July 16, 2020. https://www.state.gov/independent-states-in-the-world/.

93. Fry, Richard; Parker, Kim. "Early Benchmarks Show 'Post-Millennials' on Track to Be Most Diverse, Best-Educated Generation Yet; A demographic portrait of today's 6- to 21-year-olds." Pew Research Center. Nov. 15, 2018. https://www.pewsocialtrends.org/2018/11/15/early-benchmarks-show-post-millennials-on-track-to-be-most-diverse-best-educated-generation-yet/.

94. Watson, Amy. "Number of commercial TV stations in the United States from 1950 to 2017." Statista. Nov 21, 2019. https://www.statista.com/statistics/189655/number-of-commercial-television-stations-in-the-us-since-1950/%2C761,had%20been%20sold%20that%20year/.

95. Netter, Sarah. "Former Justice Pushing for More Civics, Less 'American Idol' Sandra Day O'Connor is pushing civics education through online games for kids." ABC News. March 4, 2009. https://abcnews.go.com/GMA/story?id=7004234&page=1/.

96. Lagemann, Ellen Condliffe. "Renewing Civic Education; Time to restore American higher education's lost mission." *Harvard Magazine*. March-April 2012. https://harvardmagazine.com/2012/03/renewing-civic-education/.

97. McCarthy, Justin. "U.S. Confidence in Organized Religion Remains Low." Gallup. July 8, 2019. https://news.gallup.com/poll/259964/confidence-organized-religion-remains-low.aspx/.

98. The Fund for American Studies 2014 Annual Report. May 1, 2015.

https://issuu.com/tfas/docs/annual_report_digital/.

99. "Pro-Democracy Leader Garry Kasparov Accepts TFAS 2017 Walter Judd Freedom Award." The Fund for American Studies. Oct. 4, 2017. https://tfas.org/news/pro-democracy-leader-garry-kasparov-accepts-tfas-2017-walter-judd-freedom-award/.

100. Buxton, Matt. "'To hell with politics.' U.S. Senate unveils portrait honoring Alaska's U.S. Sen. Ted Stevens." *The Midnight Sun*. Oct. 23, 2019. https://midnightsunak.com/2019/10/23/to-hell-with-politics-u-s-senate-unveils-portrait-honoring-alaskas-u-s-sen-ted-stevens/.

101. Drabold, Will. "Read Cory Booker's Speech at the Democratic Convention." Time. July 26, 2016. https://time.com/4421756/democratic-convention-cory-booker-transcript-speech/.

102. Rector, Robert; Menon, Vijay. "Understanding the Hidden $1.1 Trillion Welfare System and How to Reform It." The Heritage Foundation. April 5, 2018. https://www.heritage.org/welfare/report/understanding-the-hidden-11-trillion-welfare-system-and-how-reform-it/.

103. "Wartime Blackouts Were a Patriotic Duty in the 1940s." MeetAmerica. https://www.meetamerica.com/wartime-blackouts-were-a-patriotic-duty-in-the-1940s/.

104. Davenport, Kelsey. "Chronology of U.S.-North Korean Nuclear and Missile Diplomacy." Arms Control Association. July 2020. https://www.armscontrol.org/factsheets/dprkchron/.

105. "The Great Communicator|Ronald Reagan; In His Words." Reagan.com Official Blog. May 1, 2018. https://www.reagan.com/the-great-communicator-ronald-reagan/.

106. Paymar, Jim. "Speak Like a Leader." *Forbes*. Feb. 2, 2012. https://www.forbes.com/sites/jimpaymar/2012/02/02/speak-like-a-leader/#32636c5f7144/.

107. Blizzard, Brittany; Batalova, Jeanne. "Naturalization Trends in the United States." Migration Policy Institute. July 11, 2019. https://www.migrationpolicy.org/article/naturalization-trends-united-states-2017/.

108. "Citizenship Rights and Responsibilities." U.S. Citizenship and Immigration Services. April 23, 2020. https://www.uscis.gov/citizenship-resource-center/learn-about-citizenship/citizenship-and-naturalization/citizenship-rights-and-responsibilities#:~:text=Citizenship%20is%20the%20common%20thread/.

109. Rose, Joel. "The Latest Immigration Crackdown May Be Fake Social Security Numbers." NPR. March 29, 2019. https://www.npr.org/2019/

03/29/707931619/social-security-administration-plans-to-revive-no-match-letters/.

110. Kamarck, Elaine; Stenglein, Christine. "How many undocumented immigrants are in the United States and who are they?" Brookings. Nov. 12, 2019. https://www.brookings.edu/policy2020/votervital/how-many-undocumented-immigrants-are-in-the-united-states-and-who-are-they/.

111. Obama, Barack. "Remarks by the President in Address to the Nation on Immigration." Obama White House. Nov. 20, 2014. https://obamawhitehouse.archives.gov/the-press-office/2014/11/20/remarks-president-address-nation-immigration.

112. Immigration and Ethnic History Society. "Nationality Act of 1790." Immigration History. 2019. https://immigrationhistory.org/item/1790-nationality-act/.

113. History.com editors. "Alien and Sedition Acts." History. Nov. 9, 2009. https://www.history.com/topics/early-us/alien-and-sedition-acts#:~:text=The%20Alien%20and%20Sedition%20Acts%20were%20a%20series%20of%20fou r,speech%20and%20of%20the%20press.

114. Immigration and Ethnic History Society. "Immigration Act of 1864." Immigration History. 2019. https://immigrationhistory.org/item/immigration-act-of-1864/#:~:text=This%20law%20legalized%20labor%20recruitment,but%20it%20was%20quickly%20repealed.

115. "Early American Immigration Policies." U.S. Citizenship and Immigration Services. July 30, 2020. https://www.uscis.gov/about-us/our-history/overview-of-ins-history/early-american-immigration-policies#:~:text=The%20general%20Immigration%20Act%20of,for%20new%20federal%20enforcement%20authorities.

116. History.com staff. "Chinese Exclusion Act." History. Originally published Aug. 24, 2018; updated Sept. 13, 2019. https://www.history.com/topics/immigration/chinese-exclusion-act-1882.

117. Immigration and Ethnic History Society. "Scot Act of 1888." Immigration History. 2019. https://immigrationhistory.org/item/scott-act/.

118. "Ellis Island Chronology." National Park Service. Jan. 8, 2020. https://www.nps.gov/elis/learn/historyculture/ellis-island-chronology.htm.

119. Immigration and Ethnic History Society. "Geary Act (1872)." Immigration History. 2019. https://immigrationhistory.org/item/geary-act/.

120. Boissoneault, Lorraine. "Literacy Tests and Asian Exclusion Were the Hallmarks of the 1917 Immigration Act." *Smithsonian Magazine*. Feb. 6, 2017. https://www.smithsonianmag.com/history/how-america-grappled-immigration-100-

years-ago-180962058/#:~:text=The%20test%20was%20a%20part, from%20the%20%E2%80%9CAsiatic%20zone. %E2%80%9D/.

121. Immigration and Ethnic History Society. "Emergency Quota Law (1921)." Immigration History. 2019. https://immigrationhistory.org/item/%E2%80%8B1921-emergency-quota-law/.

122. Immigration and Ethnic History Society. "Immigration Act of 1924 (Johnson-Reed Act)." Immigration History. 2019. https://immigrationhistory.org/item/1924-immigration-act-johnson-reed-act/.

123. Immigration and Ethnic History Society. "Bracero Agreement (1942-1964)." Immigration History. 2019. https://immigrationhistory.org/item/bracero-agreement/.

124. Dewey, Joseph. "Immigration Act of 1943." Immigration to the United States. 2015. https://immigrationtounitedstates.org/591-immigration-act-of-1943.html/.

125. Immigration and Ethnic History Society. "War Brides Act (1945 & 1946)." Immigration History. 2019. https://immigrationhistory.org/item/war-brides-acts-1945-1947/.

126. Immigration and Ethnic History Society. "Displaced Persons Act (1948)." Immigration History. 2019. https://immigrationhistory.org/item/1948-displaced-persons-act/.

127. Immigration and Ethnic History Society. "Immigration and Nationality Act of 1952 (McCarran-Walter Act)." Immigration History. 2019. https://immigrationhistory.org/item/immigration-and-nationality-act-the-mccarran-walter-act/.

128. Immigration and Ethnic History Society. "Refugee Relief Act (1953)." Immigration History. 2019. https://immigrationhistory.org/item/1953-refugee-relief-act/.

129. "Title 22; Chapter 36—Migration and Refugee Assistance." U.S. House of Representatives Office of the Law Revision Counsel. United States Code. https://uscode.house.gov/view.xhtml?path=/prelim@title22/chapter36&edition=prelim.

130. Immigration and Ethnic History Society. "Immigration and Nationality Act of 1965 (Hart-Celler Act)." Immigration History. 2019. https://immigrationhistory.org/item/hart-celler-act/.

131. Immigration and Ethnic History Society. "Indochina Migration and Refugee Assistance Act (1975)." Immigration History. 2019. https://immigrationhistory.org/item/1975-indochina-migration-and-refugee-

assistance-act/.

132. Immigration and Ethnic History Society. "Immigration and Nationality Act Amendments of 1976 and 1978." Immigration History. 2019. https://immigrationhistory.org/item/immigration-and-nationality-act-amendments-of-1976-and-1978/.

133. Immigration and Ethnic History Society. "Refugee Act of 1980." Immigration History. 2019. https://immigrationhistory.org/item/refugee-act-of-1980/.

134. "S.1200 - Immigration Reform and Control Act of 1986; Summary: S.1200 — 99th Congress (1985-1986); Conference report filed in House." Nov. 14, 1986. https://www.congress.gov/bill/99th-congress/senate-bill/1200#:~:text= Immigration%20Reform%20and%20Control%20Act%20of%201986%20%2D%20 Title%20I%3A%20Control,employment%20any%20alien%20knowing%20that/.

135. "H.R.5210 - Anti-Drug Abuse Act of 1988; Summary: H.R.5210 — 100th Congress (1987-1988); House agreed to Senate amendment with amendment." Nov. 22, 1988. https:// www.congress.gov/bill/100th-congress/house-bill/5210.

136. "S.358 - Immigration Act of 1990; Summary: S.358 — 101st Congress (1989-1990); Conference report filed in House." Nov. 26, 1990. https://www.congress.gov/bill/101st-congress/ senate-bill/358/.

137. "H.R.3355 - Violent Crime Control and Law Enforcement Act of 1994; Text: H.R.3355 — 103rd Congress (1993-1994); Enrolled Bill." Jan. 25, 1994. https://www.congress.gov/bill/103rd-congress/house-bill/3355/text/.

138. "Illegal Immigration Reform and Immigrant Responsibility Act of 1996; Conference Report (to accompany H.R. 2202); 104th Congress." Sept. 24, 1996. https://www.congress.gov/104/crpt/ hrpt828/CRPT-104hrpt828.pdf/.

139. Immigration and Ethnic History Society. "Nicaraguan Adjustment and Central American Relief Act." Immigration History. 2019. https://immigrationhistory.org/item/nicaraguan-adjustment-and-central-american-relief-act/.

140. Immigration and Ethnic History Society. "Haitian Refugee Immigrant Fairness Act." Immigration History. 2019. https://immigrationhistory.org/item/haitian-refugee-immigrant-fairness-act/.

141. History.com editors. "George W. Bush signs the Patriot Act." History. Originally published Nov. 16, 2009; updated Oct. 23, 2020. https://www.history.com/this-day-in-history/george-w-bush-signs-the-patriot-act/.

142. "H.R.3525 - Enhanced Border Security and Visa Entry Reform Act of

2002; Summary: H.R. 3525 — 107th Congress (2001-2002); Passed Senate amended." April 18, 2002. https://www.congress.gov/bill/107th-congress/house-bill/3525/.

143. "The History of Federal Requirements for State Issued Driver's Licenses and Identification Cards; Today: Where We Stand." National Conference of State Legislatures. https:// www.ncsl.org/research/transportation/history-behind-the-real-id-act.aspx/.

144. "H.R.6061 - Secure Fence Act of 2006; Summary: H.R.6061 — 109th Congress (2005-2006); Public Law No: 109-367." Oct. 26, 2006. https://www.congress.gov/bill/109th-congress/house-bill/6061/.

145. "Independent Task Force on Immigration and America's Future: Members." Migration Policy Institute. https://www.migrationpolicy.org/programs/us-immigration-policy-program/task-force-members/.

146. von Spakovsky, Hans A. "DACA Is Unconstitutional, as Obama Admitted." The Heritage Foundation. Sept. 8, 2017. https://www.heritage.org/immigration/commentary/daca-unconstitutional-obama-admitted/.

147. Redden, Elizabeth. "Trump Ends DACA." Inside Higher Ed. Sept. 6, 2017. https://www.insidehighered.com/news/2017/09/06/trump-administration-announces-plans-wind-down-daca-after-six-months/.

148. "DACA: Frequently Asked Questions." Immigrant Legal Resource Center. Sept. 1, 2020. https://www.ilrc.org/daca-frequently-asked-questions?gclid=Cj0KCQjwwOz6BRCgARIsAKEG4FWUG4utOMzzKKONDIWUCI8NXz9As6PVcgNTgBRi dTNXA8XjKac0fJgaAsboEALw_wcB/.

149. Federation for American Immigration Reform website. https://www.fairus.org/.

150. "Immigration Reform That Will Make America Great Again." Donald J. Trump website. https://assets.donaldjtrump.com/Immigration-Reform-Trump.pdf/.

151. "Donald Trump wants to deport every single illegal immigrant - could he?" BBC. Nov. 11, 2015. https://www.bbc.com/news/world-us-canada-34789502.

152. Krogstad, Jens Manuel; Passel, Jeffrey S.; Cohn, D'Vera. "5 facts about illegal immigration in the U.S." Pew Research Center. June 12, 2019. https://www.pewresearch.org/fact-tank/2019/06/12/5-facts-about-illegal-immigration-in-the-u-s/.

153. "Road Rage Statistics - How to Avoid Rage & Stay Safe." Road & Travel Magazine. 2018-2020. https://www.roadandtravel.com/safetyandsecurity/2007/road-rage.htm/.

154. Burrows, Dan. "Millionaires in America 2020: All 50 States Ranked." Kiplinger. May 28, 2020. https://www.kiplinger.com/slideshow/investing/t006-s001-millionaires-america-all-50-states-ranked/index.html/.

155. Fry, Richard. "Millennials overtake Baby Boomers as America's largest generation." Pew Research Center. April 28, 2020. https://www.pewresearch.org/fact-tank/2020/04/28/millennials-overtake-baby-boomers-as-americas-largest-generation/.

156. "Sen. John McCain's full speech at Liberty Medal ceremony." Madison.com. June 1, 2020; updated June 8, 2020. https://madison.com/news/national/govt-and-politics/sen-john-mccains-full-speech-at-liberty-medal-ceremony/article_1f57c6f2-341c-5773-acdd-619fe2a45533.html/.

157. Fry, Richard. "Americans are moving at historically low rates, in part because millennials are staying put." Pew Research Center. Feb. 13, 2017. https://www.pewresearch.org/fact-tank/2017/02/13/americans-are-moving-at-historically-low-rates-in-part-because-millennials-are-staying-put/.

158. Povoledo, Elizabeth. "Teenagers, Forget Engineering. Your Future Is Craft." *The New York Times*. Oct. 19, 2018. https://www.nytimes.com/2018/10/19/fashion/italy-youth-unemployment-fendi-craftsmanship.html?auth=login-google1tap&login=google1tap/.

159. Morellos, Alexandros. "7 Top Futurists Make Some Pretty Surprising Predictions About What The Next Decade Will Bring." Science of Singularity. May 26, 2015. https://scienceofsingularity.com/2015/05/26/7-top-futurists-make-some-pretty-surprising-predictions-about-what-the-next-decade-will-bring/.

# INDEX

*1776*, 35, 46, 57, 59, 60, 80, 120, 153
*9/11*, 2, 24, 29, 32, 35, 137

## A

A Crucible Moment, 22
ABC News, 92, 95, 159
Adam and Eve, 15
Adams, Abigail, 66, 158
Adams, John, 59, 61, 66
Affordable Care Act, 96
Afghanistan, 17, 31, 47, 51, 79, 142, 152
African Americans, 63, 69
American democracy, 11, 72, 85, 86, 89, 92, 104, 105, 108
American Enterprise Institute, 18, 151
American flag, 18, 25, 34, 35, 51, 60, 71, 72, 111, 156
American military, 30, 54, 57
American University, 17, 151
American citizenship, 11, 53, 55, 74, 84, 89, 106, 108, 109, 111, 115, 128
American Constitution, 21
Amsterdam, 28
Anthony, Susan B., 66, 158

anthropologists, 15
antislavery forces, 62
antiwar activists, 47
Ardi, 15
Arizona, 4, 13, 17, 140
attack (1/6/21) on Capitol, 46
authority, 30, 53, 55, 59, 131

## B

Baby Boomers, 138, 144, 165
Battle of Bunker Hill, 17
Battle of the Bulge, 17
Bill of Rights, 47, 59-61, 76
Black Lives Matter, 158
Booker, Cory, 97
Bosnia, 28
Boston Tea Party, 46
Boy Scouts of America, 89
Bush, George W., 33, 126
Bush, George H. W., 28, 57, 140

## C

call to patriotic action, 7, 134
CATO Institute, 131

CBS, 18
CBS/*New York Times* poll, 18
Center for Civic Education, 19
Chesterton, G. K., 23
China, 17, 21, 27, 43, 46, 124, 143, 162
Chinese laborers, 121, 122
Christian(ity), 67
Church of England, 28
citizen involvement, 74, 82
citizenship, 7, 11, 17, 18, 24, 26, 47, 53, 55, 63, 64, 74, 81, 84, 88, 89, 94, 95, 98-118, 120, 121, 127-131, 137, 138, 147, 160, 161
civic engagement, 18, 20, 83-85
civics (defined), 7, 25, 74, 90
Civil Rights Act of 1964, 63
Civil War, American, 2, 33, 40, 48, 62, 121, 156
Clinton, Hillary, 26
Clinton, Bill, 28
Cold War, 18
commitment, 12, 33, 39, 40, 48, 51, 54, 56, 72, 85, 98, 108, 141, 148
Congress, 4, 9, 23, 26, 36, 37, 40, 47, 48, 63, 64, 67, 77-79, 89, 92-96, 99, 102, 117-128, 131-133, 137, 149, 153, 163, 164
Constitution, 11, 17, 19, 21, 25, 36, 40, 44, 46, 47, 52, 53, 56-61, 73-76, 83, 84, 86, 90, 101, 104, 107, 108, 112, 113, 121, 122, 131, 139, 140, 142, 144, 156, 164
Constitutional Convention, 40
Continental Congress, 40
cryptocurrencies, 143

Cuba, 2, 28, 32, 43, 99, 124, 126

# D

DACA, 111, 116, 118, 119, 128, 129, 131, 132, 164
Daniels, Mitch, 38
Daughters of the American Revolution, 113
Declaration of Independence, 19, 28, 44, 47, 60, 61, 104
Deferred Action for Childhood Arrivals, 116, 128
Delaware River, 35
Democracy Commission, 12
Democrat(s), 50, 64, 95, 96, 97, 128, 149
Democratic, 23, 24, 38, 43, 50, 69, 82, 86, 96, 97, 105, 107, 160
dissent, 7, 59-63, 66-70, 72, 73, 156
Domino Theory, 64

# E

East Africa, 15
Eighteenth Amendment, 36, 67
Eisenhower, Dwight D., 37, 65, 153
electoral college, 52
Ellis Island, 32, 111
engagement, 18, 20, 23, 48, 53, 54, 74, 83-85, 156
England, 28, 60
Europe, 27, 28, 31, 123, 124

## F

First Amendment, 36, 46, 67, 86
Flag Day, 34
flag(s), 18, 25, 29, 34, 35, 49, 51, 60, 71-73, 102, 111, 152, 156
Florida, 22, 56
Foreign Affairs, 31, 55, 80, 156
founding fathers, 21, 25, 29, 49, 59, 93, 96
Franklin, Benjamin, 61
free speech, 59, 60, 70, 73
freedom, 11, 12, 25, 28, 30, 32-34, 36, 37, 39, 41, 43-46, 50, 53, 54, 56, 57, 60, 61, 73, 75, 76, 79, 80, 90, 92, 98, 107, 109-111, 115, 134, 135, 145, 155, 157, 160

## G

Gallup poll(s), 18, 20, 50, 152, 156, 159
Gates, Bill, 77
Gen Z(ers), 9, 17, 24, 85
Gettysburg Address, 20, 41, 153
Glenn, John, 29
God, 11, 19, 37, 41, 42, 44, 113, 153
Gorsuch, Neal, 92, 96
Great Depression, 42, 51, 138
Great Britain, 60, 61
Greece, 26
gun control, 22, 47, 56, 85, 95
gun violence, 46

## H

Haiti, 28, 99, 126, 163
Hale, Nathan, 16
Hall, Beatrice Evelyn, 25
Hamilton, Alexander, 29, 40, 61, 127
Hancock, John, 61
Harrison, Benjamin, 122
Harvard University, 13, 21, 23, 27, 51, 101
*Harvard Magazine*, 82, 159
Heck, Denny, 23
Henry, Patrick, 40, 153
Herve, Gustave, 56
*Hillbilly Elegy*, 52
history of citizenship, 7, 120
House of Representatives, 92, 93, 96, 127, 130, 162
Humphrey, Hubert, 37, 153

## I

immigrant(s), 32, 88, 89, 101, 108, 112, 113, 115-118, 120, 121, 126, 127, 132, 163, 164
immigration, 17, 18, 20, 32, 56, 88, 89, 104, 106-110, 114, 115, 117-132, 160-164
independence, 19, 28, 29, 34, 36, 37, 39, 40, 44, 47, 49, 51, 60, 61, 78, 91, 104, 156
Independence Day, 49, 51, 156
Iraq, 2, 17, 31, 47, 51, 79, 142, 152
Iwo Jima Memorial, 34, 72, 111

## J

January 6, 2021 (attack on Capitol), 46
Jefferson, Thomas, 19, 61, 75, 156
Jefferson, Charles E., 15
Jim Crow laws, 20, 64
John C. Calhoun, 70
Johnson, Lyndon B., 43
Johnson, Samuel, 56

## K

Kaepernick, Colin, 71, 72
Kennedy, John F., 43, 64, 65, 124, 154
King, Jr. Martin Luther, 29, 33, 44, 63, 155, 157
King George, 60
King James I, 28
Korea, 20, 31, 33, 77, 103, 154, 155, 160
Korean War Memorial, 33
Korean War, 33

## L

League of Women Voters, 89, 113
Lee, Robert E., 70
Lincoln, Abraham, 40, 62, 111, 121
Llosa, Mario Vargas, 12
Locknane, Duane, 71-73
London, 28
Louisiana Purchase, 61
loyalty, 52-54
Lucy, 15, 66

## M

MacArthur, Douglas, 16, 43, 155
Madison, James, 29, 40, 61, 165
Marshall, John, 61
Marshall Plan, 27, 31
Marshall, George C., 27, 152
Marx, Karl, 56
Mayflower, 28
McCain, John, 140, 141, 145
McCullouh, Thayne, 27
McDermott, Jim, 23
McHugh, John, 16
Memorial Day, 49
Mexico, 68, 123, 129, 158
Middle East, 79
militarism, 57
millennial(s), 9, 17, 24, 49-51, 85, 86, 105, 136, 138, 139, 142-144, 159, 165
Monroe Doctrine, 31, 80
Monroe, James, 31
mottoes, 37, 38, 48

## N

national solidarity, 56
National Museum of Patriotism, 48, 49
National Foundation of Patriotism, 48

National Football League (NFL), 68, 70, 71, 159
nationalism, 10, 49, 55, 156
NATO, 80
naturalization, 11, 17, 53, 100, 101, 104, 107, 108, 111, 113, 115, 120, 130, 160
naturalized citizens, 11, 108, 111, 121
Nebraska, 17
Nethercutt Foundation, 102, 106
New York, 13, 16, 18, 29, 32, 41-43, 65, 85, 111, 117, 159, 165
New World, 28
New York Harbor, 32
*New York Times, The,* 18, 65, 159, 165
*Newsweek,* 17, 18, 151
Nicaragua, 12, 126, 163
Nineteenth Amendment, 66
Nixon, Richard, 36, 43
Noonan, Peggy, 23
North American Treaty Organization (NATO), 80
North Korea, 20, 77, 103, 160
North Vietnam, 64

# O

O'Connor, Sandra Day, 95, 159
O'Malley, Martin, 69
Olympic Games, 29, 68
Olympics, 68, 158
Owens, Jesse, 29

# P

Paine, Thomas, 35, 153
Paris, 28, 118
Parkland, Florida, shooting, 56
patriotic imagery, 35
patriotism (elements of), 7, 27, 52, 55
patriotism (definition), 7, 15, 147
patriotism (essentials of), 7, 53
Pearl Harbor, 29, 42, 102, 154
Pentagon Papers, 65
Pew Research/study, 34, 152, 155, 156, 159, 164, 165
Plato, 26
Pledge of Allegiance, 51, 72
President's Day, 49
Princeton University, 70
Prohibition, 36, 57, 67, 68, 158
public platform, 53, 54

# R

reconstruction, 63
Republican Party, 42
Republican(s), 24, 26, 42, 50, 82, 95, 96, 97, 143, 149, 156
Revere, Paul, 29
Revolutionary War, 35, 51, 60, 61
Rice, Thomas O., 112
Rodgers, Cathy McMorris, 16
Roosevelt, Franklin Delano, 42
Roosevelt, Theodore, 41
Russia, 46, 92

## S

Sasse, Ben, 23
Seneca Falls Convention, 65
Shaw, George Bernard, 58
slavery, 63, 70, 159
Snider, Nicholas D., 49
social activists, 24
Socrates, 26
Sons of the American Revolution, 113
Sotomayor, Sonia, 86, 112
South Vietnam, 65
Southern whites, 63
Soviet Union, 43, 124
Stanton, Elizabeth Cady, 66
Stone, Lucy, 66
suffrage organizations, 65
Supreme Court, 11, 17, 19, 23, 60, 61, 64, 79, 81, 86, 92, 95, 122

## T

Temperance Movement, 67
*The Republic*, 42, 86
Thirteenth Amendment, 63
Tolstoy, Leo, 56
Truman, Harry, 34, 43
Trump, Donald, 20, 25, 143, 158
Twain, Mark, 12

## U

unalienable rights, 44
undocumented immigrant(s), 104, 111, 115, 116, 119, 125, 132, 161
US Department of Defense, 78
US Supreme Court, 11, 17, 19, 23, 60, 61, 64, 79, 81, 86, 92, 95, 122
US civics test, 17
US Capitol, 24
US Senate, 92-94, 96, 97, 99, 127, 128, 130, 156, 160, 163, 164
US Naturalization Act, 120
US Citizenship and Immigration Services (USCIS), 88, 89, 107-109, 111, 113, 115, 117, 127, 160, 161
US Navy, 42
Union of Soviet Socialist Republics (USSR), 32

## V

Vance, J.D., 52
victimhood, 52
Vietnam War, 17, 31, 33, 36, 64, 65, 72, 96, 157
Vietnam War Memorial, 33
Voting Rights Act of 1965, 63

## W-Y

Walden, Greg, 23
*Wall Street Journal, The,* 23
War of 1812, 78
War of American Independence (also see *Revolutionary War*), 60

Washington, George, 31, 39, 61, 70
*Washington Post, The,* 95, 151
*Washington Post*-ABC News poll, 95
Washington, DC, 17, 22, 23, 32, 48, 62, 63, 95, 140
Weldon, Felix de, 34
Welsh, Tim, 30
white supremacy, 56
White House, 22, 62, 66, 111, 154, 158, 161

Wilde, Oscar, 56

Wilson, Woodrow, 34, 37, 70, 127
Wimmer, Andreas, 55
women's right to vote, 65
World War I (WWI), 48
World War II (WWII), 17, 27, 29, 30, 33, 34, 48, 51, 72, 80, 102, 123, 138, 152
World War II Memorial, 33
YouTube, 17

# About the Author

GEORGE R. NETHERCUTT, JR. is Founder and Chairman of The George Nethercutt Civics Foundation, a nonprofit, nonpartisan organization established to foster an understanding of government and public policies and to create a new generation of principled leaders in America. He is a lawyer and from 1995-2005 repre-sented Washington State's 5th Con-gressional District as  a member of the US House of Representatives. His first book, *In Tune with America: Our History in Song* (Marquette Books), also is available through Amazon.com.

VISIT
www.nethercuttcivicsfoundation.org
and take the free civics test